ENGLISH FURNITURE

ENGLISH FURNITURE

JAMES YORKE

WHSMITH
EXCLUSIVE
· BOOKS ·

This edition produced exclusively for
W.H. Smith & Son Limited
Greenbridge Industrial Estate
Greenbridge Road
Swindon
Wiltshire SN3 3LD

Produced by
Bison Books Ltd
Kimbolton House
117A Fulham Road
London SW3 6RL

ISBN 0-86124-623-3

Printed in Hong Kong

PAGE 1 *Adjustable chair by William Morris.*
PAGE 3 *The Great Bed of Ware, about 1580.*
PAGE 4/5 *Detail of the Manxman piano designed by Hugh Baillie Scott, about 1903.*

CONTENTS

Introduction

From Master Walter of Durham to John Makepeace of Parnham, this book aims to serve as an introduction to the history of English furniture from the Middle Ages to the present. The chapters have been divided on the basis of style rather than the accessions and deaths of monarchs. Terms like 'William and Mary' or 'Queen Anne' are also convenient, however and the accession of a new king or queen could provide no small impetus to a particular style. Although the Commonwealth is now looked upon as less drab and philistine than it once was, the Restoration of Charles II and the re-establishment of the royal court in 1660 made an enormous impact on the decorative arts, No satisfactory substitute has yet been found for the term 'Victorian', despite the countless styles that made their appearance in Victoria's reign, partly because so many of them were concurrent. Changes in style are not as chronologically clear cut as the reigns of sovereigns and there is plenty of overlap: for example, the massive, classical furniture called 'Grecian' lasted from the mid-1820s until the early 1850s, spanning the reigns of George IV, William IV and Victoria. Throughout this book the emphasis is on architects and

LEFT
Claviorgan (harpsichord-cum-organ) by Lodewyk Theewes, 1579, formerly from Ightham Mote, Kent. The earliest dated English keyboard instrument to survive and a rare example of painted furniture of the time.

RIGHT
The State Bed at Nostell Priory, about 1771. The woodwork is by Thomas Chippendale and the hangings, based on surviving fragments and parallels, were made in the 1980s.

LEFT
Sidetable, with incised lacquer top and mirror stand, English or Dutch, about 1675. These are part of the original furnishings of Ham House.

RIGHT ABOVE
Marriage chest, about 1720, originally from Shobden Court, bearing the crest of Viscount Bateman and attributed to James Moore Senior. The design is loosely based on that of the sixteenth-century Italian cassone.

RIGHT BELOW
Part of a dressing table with gilt brass mounts, probably made by John Channon, a highly fashionable cabinetmaker of St Martin's Lane in about 1740.

designers, as they were the innovators who introduced the forms that cabinetmakers copied. In many cases furniture was a vital component in the design of an overall interior, whether the architect was Robert Adam or Charles Rennie Mackintosh.

By the mid thirteenth century interesting furniture begins to be documented, with the earliest surviving examples, such as the Coronation Throne of Westminster Abbey, dating from around 1300. Increasing prosperity and stability led to a requirement for more elaborate furniture, with France and Flanders, countries closely linked with England, serving as models for luxury and elegance. The Tudors saw the first hesitant introduction of Renaissance style, the first stages of which were cut short by the Reformation and the break with the church of Rome. However, the introduction of the printing press led to the spread and consolidation of classically based ornament through the architectural works of Serlio and Northern European pattern books. The genius of Inigo Jones introduced the architecture of Andrea Palladio to the court of the first two Stuart kings, James I and Charles I, and began to bring the arts of England out of their provincial backwater in the process. In this he was helped by Francis Clein, the Danish painter and tapestry designer.

LEFT
State Drawing Room, Kedleston, including armchairs in the neoclassical style, and the Merman Sofas, designed by John Linnell in about 1762 and executed by his workshop in about 1765.

BELOW
Armchair and footstool, English, about 1640, formerly the property of Archbishop Juxon and said to have been used by Charles I at his trial in 1649.

Under Charles II, the French Baroque fashions of the court of Louis XIV became influential; architects such as Hugh May and Sir Christopher Wren worked in a style similar to that of contemporary France, rather than lagging twenty years or so behind.

At the same time foreign upholsterers like John Casbert were busy refurnishing royal palaces (even if the king was slow to pay) and cabinetmakers such as Gerrit Jensen were producing pieces, often in marquetry, of unprecedented virtuosity. The influx of French Protestant refugees following the Revocation of the Edict of Nantes added further impetus to the Baroque in England, as did the extravagant interior designs of Daniel Marot, architect to William III and himself a Huguenot. Until the last decade of the seventeenth century the majority of cabinetmakers were foreign, but increasing numbers of Englishmen were mastering the art.

The eighteenth century is usually regarded as the Golden Age of English furniture. William Kent, the able lieutenant to the great Palladian architect Lord Burlington, designed buildings, interiors and furniture to go with them. Rococo fashions were introduced from France and spread through the pattern books and engraved plates of Thomas and Batty Langley and Mathias Lock. In the late 1750s the Neoclassical style made its first appearance from France, through architects like Sir William Chambers, James 'Athenian' Stuart and Robert Adam, who remodeled the interiors of existing houses and made detailed furniture designs. The pattern books of George Hepplewhite and Thomas Sheraton popularized this style.

The Regency style is very much associated with

George, Prince of Wales, who was made Prince Regent in 1810. It originated in his refurbishment of Carlton House on coming of age in 1785 and faded away in the reign of his brother, William IV. In this period classical furniture, which owed its decoration to ancient Greek rather than Roman models, coexisted with the Gothic and Egyptian styles.

The reign of Queen Victoria was marked by large international exhibitions, where manufacturers, upholsterers and cabinetmakers exhibited their wares and vied for medals, and produced historical styles including Gothic and the serpentine curves of the Rococo revival, which were rather more popular with upholsterers. In about 1861 William Morris formed his own company, which sold wallpapers, textiles and furniture designed by himself and his friends and associates, such as Ford Madox Brown, Philip Webb and Edward Burne-Jones. These furnishings went hand in hand with the Aesthetic Movement and the 'Queen Anne' houses of Kensington and Bedford Park, built by Norman Shaw. Morris's lectures

LEFT ABOVE

Four chairs, an etching from A New Book for Chinese and Modern Chairs, by Mathias Darly, 1750.

LEFT BELOW

Gilt console table, with gilt gesso decoration on the top, by James Pascal, 1745, part of the original furnishings of Temple Newsham.

RIGHT

Barometer, thermometer and clock, giltwood, about 1730.

LEFT
Giltwood armchair from Uppark of about 1755-60 with tapestry upholstery. The subject on the chairback is taken from Francis Barlow's illustrations to Aesop's Fables.

BELOW
Stool, part of a suite of furniture made for James II by Thomas Roberts in 1688, from the Venetian Ambassador's Bedroom Suite at Knole.

and writings on design and socialism, largely inspired by his abhorrence of the Machine Age and the poverty and degradation that went with it, greatly influenced the younger generation of designers, who formed groups like the Century Guild and the Arts and Crafts Movement. They placed their emphasis on handicrafts and traditional skills, and in many cases espoused the rural way of life. Avant-garde designers such as Arthur Mackmurdo and Charles Voysey were among the originators of the Art Nouveau style, although they tended to disassociate themselves from its later continental form. Charles Rennie Mackintosh, founder of the 'Glasgow School' and famous for his highly original elongated forms, was much praised on the continent, particularly in Germany and Austria.

Furniture of the years following World War I tended to be rather conservative; the Modernist movement that had established itself in France and Germany in the early 1920s did not appear in England until the end of that decade. During the 1930s Marcel Breuer, who as a member of the Bauhaus movement had pioneered the use of

LEFT
Tripod table designed by Thomas Hope, and featured in Household Furniture and Interior Decoration, published in 1807; part of the furnishings of Hope's country residence at Deepdene, Surrey.

BELOW
Commode by Thomas Chippendale for Harewood House, 1773, in satinwood and other woods, executed by Edwin Lascelles.

tubular steel, designed pieces made of bent plywood for Jack Pritchard's firm Isokon. One of the earliest English designers to exploit tubular steel was Denham MacLaren. At the same time the arts and crafts tradition continued under Peter Waals and Sir Gordon Russell. The latter went on to design 'Utility' furniture for the Board of Trade during World War II. This was practical and cheap but well made and in the Modernist style, and an example of government-regulated furniture design. The post-war years were marked by exhibitions such as 'Britain Can Make It' and 'The Festival of Britain', and designers like Ernest Race and Robin Day came to the fore. The 1960s were synonymous with Pop culture, and furniture was no exception. Synthetic materials like acrylic and fibre glass resulted in unprecedented freedom of design and instant impact, with Peter Murdoch designing paper chairs and David Colwell the acrylic 'Contour' chair. The 1970s and 1980s were marked by a craft revival, one of its main exponents being John Makepeace of the Parnham school, and by Post-Modernist furniture designs such as those of American architect Charles Jencks.

This rapid survey of the contents of the chapters provides an introduction to the history of furniture. There is a far wider choice of material for study than was the case thirty years ago. Ralph Edwards' monumental *Dictionary of English Furniture* is a pioneering work, going into every detail of English furniture up to the 1820s. Although inventories are copiously quoted, eighteenth-century pieces of furniture are still seen as individual antiques, rather than components of a complete interior. The re-

LEFT
'Thebes' stool, produced by Liberty's in about 1880, based on an ancient Egyptian stool at the British Museum.

BELOW
Spine Chair by André Charles Dubreuil, 1988.

searches of Mark Girouard into the historic house and of John Cornforth and Peter Thornton into the interior have very much increased our awareness as to how the house worked and how the furniture was used. During the 1960s the enthusiasm for Victorian furniture that had previously been confined to a few eccentrics became a serious academic study, and in the 1970s twentieth-century furniture became an equally popular subject. This book is intended as an introduction to an exciting and rapidly expanding field.

LEFT
Sideboard in the Japanese style, by E W Godwin, 1867, reflecting the vogue for all things Japanese following the opening up of the country to the outside world in the 1850s.

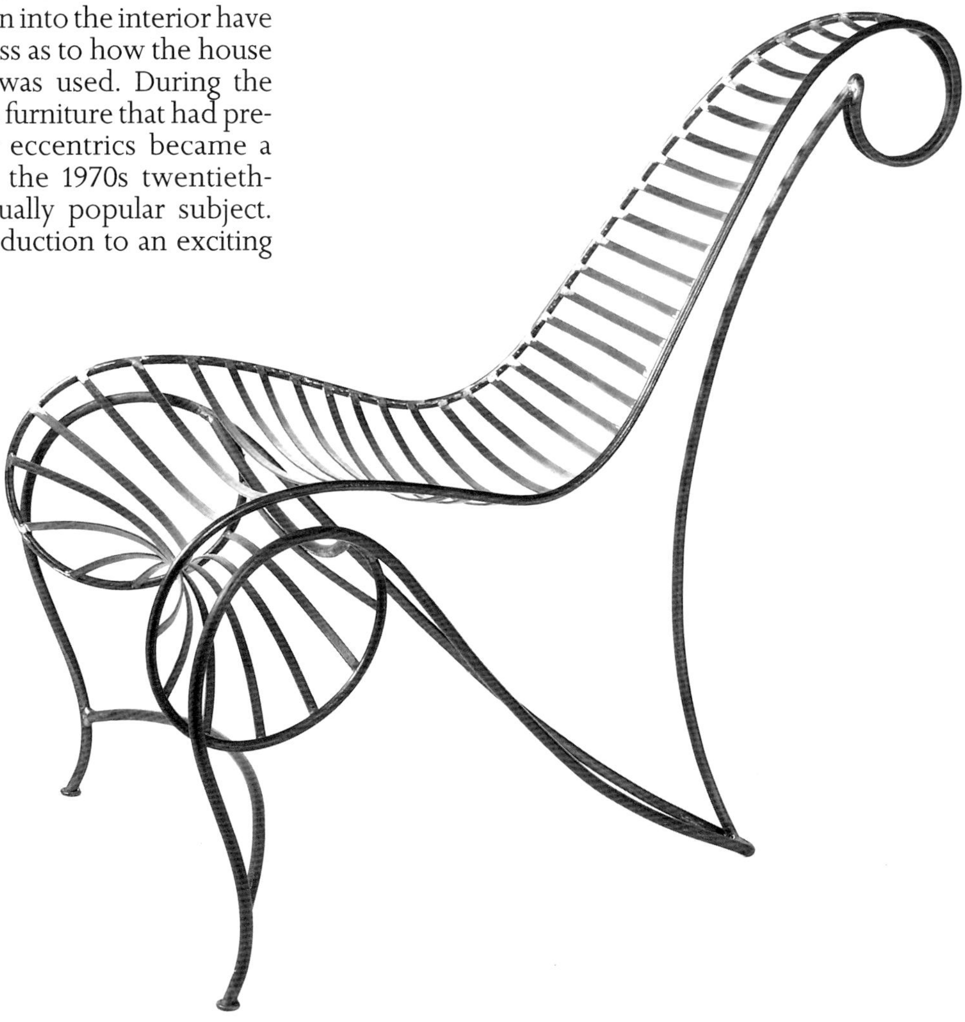

CHAPTER 1

Middle Ages

Gothic

THE HISTORY of medieval furniture does not start with one dramatic event or example. Without resorting to clichés about 'shrouds of mystery' or 'the dim distant past', it is a fact that very little documented furniture survives from before about 1300 and few references of importance have come to light before about 1240. The Coronation Throne, also known as St Edward's Throne, of Westminster Abbey, although hacked about by later generations – the pinnacles at the side were sawn off before the coronation of George IV in 1821 – was made around 1300, and the earliest record of a four-poster state bed was one made for King Henry III some time between 1242 and 1247.

Conditions in medieval England were often unstable, with the king and barons vying with each other for power. The baron's effectiveness largely depended on his enormous household of gentlemen, yeomen and grooms, and his castles and lands. His possessions frequently sported a coat-of-arms and served to enhance his status rather than reflect his tastes. The higher-ranking clergy also had enormous households, and were no less concerned with power and prestige than their secular counterparts. Both nobility and clergy had to move with their large household from one property to the next, taking with them furnishings that could easily be transported and assembled. Furniture mostly served as a vehicle for elaborate furnishings and was often no more than a basic frame, although more prestigious pieces like the throne or chair of office could receive lavish attention. Gothic ornament dominated architecture, as well as textiles and metalwork, from the middle of the twelfth century. However, as Pugin was to find out, furniture of this period was by no means all pinnacles but largely remained remarkably simple. As far as we can tell, the elaborate tracery usually associated with Gothic architecture featured mainly on thrones from the thirteenth century onward and grander chests from the 1400s.

Increasing prosperity, largely derived from the wool trade, led to the development of a town and merchant

FAR LEFT
Carved coffer with knights tilting, English or French, about 1350.

LEFT
Portrait of a scribe at his desk from an English manuscript of about 1150; note the Romanesque arcading.

class with the money and the inclination for domestic comfort. Unlike the nobility, they were less preoccupied with keeping their lands and inherited status intact. One of the most fertile areas for information about late medieval furniture is the interiors that feature in religious paintings of the fifteenth-century Netherlandish masters such as Jan Van Eyck and Robert Campin, where the Virgin Mary is often placed in a snug middle-class interior, with Joseph plying his trade as a prosperous carpenter. Connections between England and Flanders were very close at the time, mainly through the wool trade, and the Dukes of Burgundy, who had acquired this traditionally prosperous part of the continent, held a court most worth emulating. In 1363 King John II of France gave the duchy of Burgundy to his son, Philip the Bold, who married Margaret, heiress of Flanders, Artois and Franche Comté. Connections between the French and English courts had been close since 1066, no doubt helped by the fact that they both spoke French. Furthermore, in 1420, five years after the Battle of Agincourt, Henry V was in a position to declare France a dependency of the English crown. There were therefore close links between England, France and the Netherlands.

Few pieces of English medieval furniture survive and those that do either have later additions or have been cobbled together from other redundant examples with reusable parts – for example a bench end or two can come in handy for making a chair. The gaps in our know-

ledge are partly compensated for by surviving accounts, inventories and illustrations. Accounts, particularly royal ones, as well as telling us what was ordered and why, often come up with the name of a craftsman. Inventories throw light on the contents of a building, their positions, their uses, and occasionally their appearance. In adopting a more realistic approach to detail, miniaturists and painters, particularly the Netherlandish masters, provided increasingly reliable illustrations from around the 1350s onwards. That still leaves us little extant furniture and what does survive tends to be confined to churches and abbeys, the largest pieces being mainly classified as fixtures and fittings. The furniture belonging to a cathedral or abbey tended to remain in one building, where it was used for seating, storage and various liturgical purposes and, unlike the private possessions of the nobility and clergy, seldom if ever had to move from one property to another. Hence it could be and often was monumental, adding grandeur to religious ceremonies.

In unsettled conditions furniture has to be transportable, and in most European languages, from classical times onward, has been called 'moveables,' deriving from the latin *mobilia*. The most convenient furniture for containing valuables was a chest; all too necessary when banking was still fairly primitive and security was often determined in crude physical terms. Robust by necessity, these have survived in the largest numbers. Furniture tended to be looked upon as a frame for, say, luxurious bed clothes and to be discarded once the textiles had worn away, and wardrobes removed as the fashion in domestic interiors changed. There do survive a few items of prestigious furniture, such as the ecclesiastical throne of Hereford Cathedral (about 1200), an elaborate piece decorated with characteristically rounded Romanesque arcading, and the Courtfield Cradle (about 1500), a horizontally grooved box held by eagle-surmounted uprights. A number of chests with figurative illustration, like that with two knights jousting, or flamboyant late Gothic tracery on the front have also come down to us. These were heavily influenced if not actually made by French craftsmen, who had developed the most refined and intricate forms of Gothic, culminating in what is called the

Flamboyant Style of about 1500.

Surviving secular pieces of furniture tend to be later than their religious counterparts. The more widespread use of Gothic ornament, through renewed French influences, certainly made them more attractive and worth preserving but the development of urban prosperity, as well as the increased sophistication, comfort and settled conditions that went with it, were more conducive to the making of comparatively elaborate furniture by joiners and carpenters, who were by now forming their guilds. The London upholsterers and joiners had some form of organization by the fourteenth century and the carpenters by the fifteenth. There was probably a great deal of overlap between the two trades and doubtless frictions as well; disputes were to become more acrimonious during the sixteenth and seventeenth centuries and resulted in stricter regulations by the 1630s.

There are instances of furniture being made by artists. Walter of Durham, the King's sergeant painter, painted and carved a chair for Edward I, quite probably the surviving St Edward's Throne, and presumably designed it as well. This is an architectural piece with a Gothic gable surmounted by crocketing, a form of protruding foliate decoration, and the remains of pinnacles at the back and Gothic arcading at the sides. It is thought to have been covered with mosaic originally, but later painting and the subsequent removal of the paint have only left fragments of gesso from the original decoration. In France and Burgundy, artists such as Villard de Honnecourt and Melchior Broederlam designed furniture, and the making of a cradle of state called for a top-calibre painter such as Jehan d'Orleans.

Edward IV, whose sister Marguerite of York married Charles the Bold in 1468, strove to emulate the Burgundian court, the most fashionable in Europe, and requested a written description of it from Olivier de la Marche, which took the form of *L'Etat de la Maison du Duc Charles de Bourgogne*. The Burgundian court based their

LEFT
Two misericords from St Nicholas, King's Lynn, about 1419. The top one depicts a cleric at prayer and the bottom one a master carver at work.

RIGHT
Ecclesiastical chair from Hereford Cathedral, about 1200; note the Romanesque arcading at the front.

etiquette on that of France, and elaborate descriptions of feasts and ceremonies have come down to us through Olivier de la March and also Alienor de Poictiers' *Les Honneurs de la Cour*, an account of the correct furnishings for the chambers of ladies of the nobility during childbirth. Olivier de la Marche tells us at what stages trestle tables were put up and then removed at banquets and Alienor de Poictiers informs us that a state bed's function could be purely ceremonial and not to be slept in ('and the bed was made and covered with a counterpain, like a bed on which nobody sleeps'). As well as listing the hangings of the various beds she refers to the grand state cradle, lined with ermine that should reach the ground.

The most prestigious pieces of furniture, or in fact 'vehicles of furnishing,' were buffets or 'cupboards' in the original sense of the word; chairs, particularly thrones; and state beds. The buffet or cupboard was originally a board or a series of boards used for displaying plate and serving wine. John Russell, Marshal and Usher to Humphrey, Duke of Gloucester, in his *The Boke of Nurture* commands his reader 'Son, when thy souereignes table is drest in thus array, . . . than emperialle thy Cuppeborde with Siluer & gild fulle gay . . . '. Unlike the dresser, which tended to be confined to the service area, the cupboard was usually placed in the Great Hall, where entertaining of a more formal nature took place, and was covered with textiles. These shelves could be rectangular, triangular and on at least one occasion round. By the late Middle Ages, the number of shelves on a buffet indicated the status of the owner. Alienor de Poictiers reinforces the point about the hierarchy of the stepped buffet, informing us that the Queen of France and Marie of Burgundy had one with five stages, Isabelle of Portugal one with four and the Countess of Amiens one with three. At the Feast of the Pheasant that took place in Lille in 1454 the Duke of Burgundy had a buffet of six stages, while Henry VII of England used one of ten stages at a banquet at Richmond Palace.

The throne, as one would expect, and to a lesser extent the chair, was a highly symbolic piece of furniture. Shopkeepers and even peasants could possess chairs but their use was often governed by order of precedence; for example, in his own home the peasant had the right to the chair, which he would give up to someone of superior status. Should he visit the Lord in his Manor he would sit on a stool, if indeed he was allowed to sit at all. The seat traditionally represented authority, and was further enhanced by the use of a footstool and cushion. By sitting enthroned on a raised dais, the seated figure, be he king, nobleman or prelate, could dominate and be seen. The effect was increased if he sat on a sumptuous throne like, say, St Edward's Throne in Westminster Abbey, which was originally gilt and decorated with glass mosaic, or the 'marble seat' raised upon a dais at the south end of Westminster Hall used by Edward IV and Richard III. Thrones could be painted, and one such was made for Queen Margaret's (consort of Edward I) visit to the Bishop of Winchester's castle at Wolvesley. Royal accounts refer to one example 'joined with gilded and silvered nails' and made by 'Master Michael of Canterbury and a master carpenter named Reginald'.

It would seem that in rooms such as chambers upholstered chairs were used, the normal materials being

leather, cloth, padding and gilt nails (assuming the owner was fairly grand!); a red velvet chair is recorded in Henry V's inventory. The chamber served as something approaching a bed-sitting-room, where both sexes met in a more refined atmosphere than the boisterous hall, where the lord feasted with the male members of his household. He might sit on a throne with a cushion, but those at less elevated tables tended to sit on simple forms. Comfort, while not taking precedence, could at least play a more prominent role in more intimate surroundings.

The X-framed chair, which harked back to the Roman magistrate's chair, was associated with kings and bishops. This piece of furniture was used as a motif on the seals of the kings of France (Philippe I to Charles VII) and Pope Boniface IX. An entry in the Westminster Abbey inventory (1388) introduces a note of hierarchy in the form of 'Three Bishop's seats, one being silvered, the second and third iron.' Status could be further enhanced by placing a canopy above the chair. A 1252 account orders 'a canopy (tabernaculum) above the king's chair in the Hall', in the royal palace at Woodstock.

August and symbolic as X-framed chairs were, seating built with posts or boards allowed for greater variety. An important example of a boarded chair or rather bench in situ is at Mulcheney Abbey, which is very similar to a pair of seats of about 1500 with the arms of Rigaud d'Aurelhe in the Musée des Arts Décoratifs in Paris. Even allowing for a great deal of stylization in early manuscript illustrations, they can be surprisingly realistic. The Romanesque arcading of the Hereford Cathedral Chair can be found in Scandinavian examples and also in a twelfth-century English manuscript illustration of a scribe at his desk.

The state bed was a large, obtrusive piece of furniture and an excellent vehicle for luxurious textiles that displayed the wealth and status of the owner. Comments like 'convenable for her estate' or 'in conformity with his position. . .' frequently recur in inventories. Perhaps the earliest reference to a state bed is to one made for Henry III at Westminster Palace, with posts painted green with gold stars (a Master William was paid 20 marks for painting it). Although Henry III used canopy posts, the more common practice in the late Middle Ages was to suspend the canopy with iron rods from the ceiling. Rectangular canopies were called 'celours' and the conical or pyramidal versions 'sparvers'. The use of posts to support the canopy re-emerged at the beginning of the sixteenth century. The size of the canopy and whether it was a whole or a demi-celour was a mark of privilege and used to denote honor, although the whole celour was not reserved exclusively for kings. Such a bed features in Jan Van Eyck's Arnolfini marriage portrait.

LEFT

Coronation Throne from Westminster Abbey, about 1300, by Master Walter of Durham. The lions were added by Richard Roberts, son of the famous upholsterer Thomas Roberts, in 1727.

BELOW

Livery cupboard doors from the fifteenth century, with flamboyant tracery characteristic of the period.

RIGHT

Portrait of Richard II enthroned in Westminster Abbey, about 1395. Note the flamboyant decoration of the throne, particularly the pinnacles.

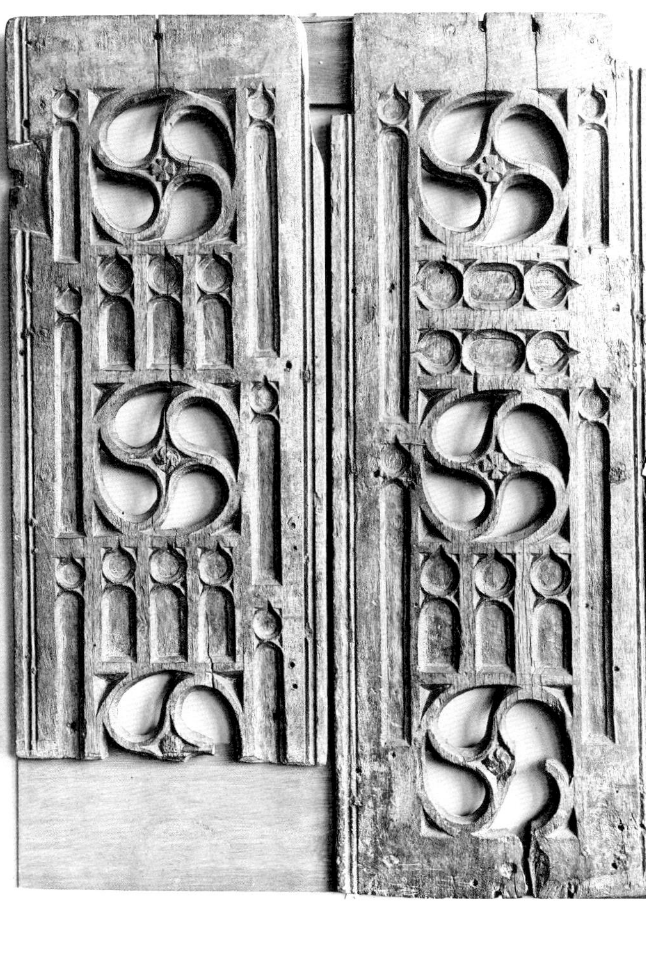

Beds denoted status and were also ceremonial often to the point of not being intended to be slept on; Alienor de Poictiers was not referring to an isolated act of eccentricity when she mentioned a bed on which 'nobody lies'. Charles the Bold had a *chambrette* where he slept and a *salette de reception* where he held state, even though that room had a state bed. Justus Van Ghent in his *Adoration of the Magi* depicts the Virgin Mary sitting on a fully made state bed, as if it were a glorified throne. Even if beds were not always used for sleep, 'trussing beds' or folding beds

ABOVE Carved chest front from about 1450, depicting scenes from the life of the Virgin. The same theme appears on English fourteenth-century needlework.

certainly were. They may have been lower versions of beds but they could have hangings and celours that matched, like John of Gaunt's '. . . other beds made for my personal use, called in England "trussing beds", with hangings and other appurtenances'. Trussing beds were presumably simple structures that came apart and could be 'trussed up' on a pack horse for travel. Although none have survived, it has been suggested that they might have resembled a seventeenth-century Swedish field bed in the Nordiska Museet, Stockholm. Most people would have had to make do with a straw mattress and a pallet. The Abbot of Durham had 'night chairs', which may have resembled the seventeenth-century day bed or sleeping chair.

Cradles could be highly ornate, particularly if they were to contain the infants of the powerful. One of the most ornate examples to survive is the cradle used for the birth of Philip the Fair or Marguerite of Austria. Their mother was Marie of Burgundy and their father Maximilian of Austria, hence the highly calligraphic M initials. Perhaps the only known English survival is the Courtfield Cradle, which has been traditionally associated with Henry V although this is open to doubt. It is richly carved, as befitted an item of furniture belonging to an important if not necessarily royal family.

Although a marble table featured in the Great Hall at Westminster during the coronation of Richard II, tables tended to be simple boards of wood, usually oak or pine, either fixed permanently and described as 'sleeping' or 'dormant' or supported on trestles, thus easily removed when not required. The layout in grand halls was similar to that still used in Oxford and Cambridge colleges. The lord's table was elevated on a dais and those of lower rank were placed at right angles at tables going the length of the hall. Two tables with cruciform trestles, wide at the top and bottom and narrow in the middle, survive at Penshurst Place, Kent. Henry IV had one 'in three sections

BELOW Desk or cupboard of about 1380. The lockplate and bookledge are post-medieval. The lion masks are similar to those on misericords in Lincoln Cathedral (c. 1370). The lower panels and base are missing.

FAR RIGHT Armchair from about 1540. Note the linenfold panels, characteristic of Netherlandish decoration from the 1450s onward (and English of a little later) and the classical figures in the back rest. This is an early example of Romayne decoration in England.

with three . . . trestles, of wood plated with silver gilt, worked and enameled with various figures of Spanish work'. Some tables could fold into smaller units, and were called folding tables; John Bishop of Dromore possessed '*unum faldingbord*'!

Perhaps the most imposing pieces of medieval furniture to survive are armoires. They are still in situ in ecclesiastical buildings such as the Zouche chapel at York Minster, the watching loft at St Albans and the Muniment Room at Wells Cathedral. The Zouche chapel armoire, a somewhat architectural piece that was probably executed in about 1500, has a crenelated cornice similar to Lord Percy's tomb of 1415 in the Fitzalan Chapel at Arundel Castle. The armoire was an integral part of town houses, being either free standing or fitted into the wall, often of an adjoining property. It could simply be shelved or unshelved storage space, but acquired doors, drawers and in some cases pigeon holes at a later stage. Open shelves that enabled both storage and display were not unknown. Because the main purpose of armoires was storage, they acquired all manner of roles ranging from bookcase to larder. They contained jewels, clothes, church vestments (hence their continued use in churches) and documents.

Chests and coffers, the other principal form of storage, were in many cases stronger and could also travel; an important consideration in restless, unstable times. They are commonly found in inventories and survive in larger numbers than any other form of medieval furniture. Terms like 'coffers' and 'standards' were fairly loosely used by medieval clerks but it would seem that coffers were used for travel, while in at least one description a standard was a leather box with a domed lid (enabling the rain to slide off while in transit). The chest was more of a strong box and used for storing money, plate, and expensive textiles. As a result it often had more than one lock, the Common Chest of Guildhall, a massive iron chest with an arched top of about 1427, having as many as six. In this case there were three hasps for padlocks and three keyholes. Locks and hasps of a later date are often evident on surviving examples, all too often as a result of a lost key and the old lock having to be forced open. Surviving examples often appear crude, being slabs of wood put together or just hollowed out. However, iron bindings could provide an opportunity for decoration. Security was the most important consideration but surviving chests from the fifteenth century onward seem to have taken on a more than purely utilitarian role, with their fronts decorated with flamboyant Gothic tracery, like the Romsey Abbey chest, or figurative carving, like the St George and the dragon chests at York Minster. Paneled chests, frequently depicted in Netherlandish paintings, appeared at the end of the fifteenth century, an example surviving at Brasenose College, Oxford.

In most cases, wooden furniture was not considered important enough for elaborate decoration. It was the plate rather than the cupboard, and the hangings rather than the bed, that displayed wealth and status. However, by about 1500 surface decoration of furniture became more elaborate and Gothic tracery became more intricate, particularly on chests. The linenfold began to be used on paneled furniture, such as headboards to beds, chairs, doors and wall paneling; the term is used to describe a sylized folded drapery motif, which originated in the Netherlands in about 1450. The headboard of the bed in Hugo Van der Goes's *Death of the Virgin* is an early example. One of its earliest appearances in England is on the door of the Audley Chapel, Hereford Cathedral, built between 1492 and 1502. This motif was to become more widespread in the sixteenth century. A linenfold paneled chair in the Victoria and Albert Museum, London, also has antique putti and scrolls – new Italian-derived blending with late Gothic motifs.

The Middle Ages were restless and unsettled but life became less primitive as the centuries progressed. Trade, largely based on wool, generated more widespread wealth in the towns, particularly the cathedral cities and market towns. Quite a number of London merchants were probably able to live in the style of Giovanni Arnolfini, depicted in Jan Van Eyck's famous marriage portrait; even a Cecilia Rose, widow of a clerk, had a 'wooden bedstead of bord, with curtains etc'. On a more elevated level, wealth and its ability to enhance the status of the lord had their part to play as much as prowess in battle. As Georges Chastellain wrote, 'After the deeds and exploits of war, which are claims to glory, the household is the first thing that strikes the eye and which it is therefore most necessary to conduct and arrange well'.

CHAPTER 2

Tudor to Commonwealth

Renaissance to Restoration

FROM ABOUT the beginning of the sixteenth century until well into the seventeenth, English craftsmen made hesitant steps toward a new style of decoration based on classical architecture. England's position on the fringes of north-west Europe meant that the new developments in Italy took longer to filter through, and Henry VIII's break with the church of Rome in 1529, coupled with the rise of Protestantism, could only hinder the process. However, the printing press spread not only the doctrines of Luther and Calvin (often accompanied with highly decorative title pages and end pieces), but also, among other things, pattern books of classical ornament, and in some cases furniture design, throughout northern Europe from about 1540 onward. The abundance of surface decoration could be and indeed was applied to English furniture, and designs for whole beds and tables began to be copied from about the 1560s onwards.

FAR LEFT
Differents Pourctraits de Menuiserie by Hans Vredeman de Vries, about 1588.

LEFT
Detail of a table at Ham House, about 1650. The female terms are like those in Inigo Jones's design for a monument to Lady Cotton in St Chad, Norton-in-Hales, of about 1611. If Inigo Jones had designed any furniture it might have looked something like this.

RIGHT
Writing box belonging to Henry VIII, from about 1525, an example of the extravagantly decorated royal possessions of the time.

Inigo Jones, the leading royal architect, and Francis Clein may have been popular in the rarified court circles around Charles I but English furniture largely retained its bulky medieval appearance until the Civil War. However, style and decoration became more refined after about 1610; while some table legs remained bulbous, others became more slender and rectangular, and the Ionic capital, often with highly exaggerated scrolls, was joined by the

more simple Doric order. The legs of English stools and chairs were simple and cylindrical, turned on a lathe with rings added for decoration and called 'turned stools', until the early seventeenth century. Then what were called 'joined stools' made their appearance, usually in the form of slim balusters joined at the base by stretchers. A more elegant version had legs in the form of Doric columns. Massive, somewhat barbarously ornate beds with wooden testers gave way to elegant French beds, simple rectangular frames covered with textiles, from about 1630. The seating furniture illustrated in *Parisian Interiors* engraved by Abraham Bosse in about 1640, with its elegant legs and uprights in the form of Doric columns, is to be found in surviving examples from England.

The term Renaissance means rebirth, in particular the revival of the study of the art, architecture, literature and philosophy of Ancient Greece and Rome. The earliest signs of this revival were to be found in Florence in about 1400, and spread throughout the leading cities of Italy by about 1480. King Charles VIII's invasion of Italy in 1490 to reassert the claim of the French crown to the kingdom of Naples resulted, among other things, in his bringing back some 22 craftsmen including Domenico da Cortona and Bernardo da Brescia, two workers in *intarsia*, a highly skilled form of inlay, developed in Italy from the fourteenth century. Francis I (1515 – 1547) sustained the royal enthusiasm for all things Italian, employing Francesco Primaticcio and Rosso Fiorentino from about 1530 to decorate his palace at Fontainebleau in the Mannerist style, a more ornate and contrived version of Renaissance decoration which had developed in Italy by about 1510. Mannerist decoration drew its inspiration largely from the 'grotesque' a term derived from the Italian word for cave. These extravagant motifs originated with Roman wall paintings particularly the wall decorations of the *Domus Aurea*, the palace of the Emperor Nero, rediscovered at the end of the fifteenth century.

The style that Primaticcio and Fiorentino introduced to France became known as the School of Fontainebleau, and helped supplant all things Gothic in that country. To European craftsmen, whether French, German, Netherlandish or English, trained in the Gothic idiom, this new extravagant form of classical decoration was far easier to assimilate, as a substitute for Gothic tracery, than the pure antique decorations of Brunelleschi or other Florentine

LEFT *English armchair, about 1535, the back carved with Renaissance ornament.*

ABOVE *Wendel Dietterlin's design for a gate in* Architectura, *c 1600. Included in these fantastic designs are strapwork motifs which were to become widespread throughout northern Europe in the early seventeenth century.*

ABOVE RIGHT *Armchair of about 1560, known as the 'Glastonbury Chair' after one in the Bishop's Palace at Wells, said to have come from Glastonbury Abbey.*

BELOW RIGHT *English inlaid chest, about 1580, probably made by German craftsmen in Southwark who borrowed ideas from Hans Vredeman de Vries and others.*

architects of the mid-fifteenth century. Mannerist motifs, including cupids, masks, scrolls and free adaptations of architectural motifs, were surface decoration that could easily be applied to Gothic forms, including furniture. Mastering the purer Florentine version would have required a new architectural language and access to abundant ancient ruins, in good condition.

The Italian Renaissance first appeared in England when Henry VII commissioned a tomb from Piero Torrigiani, an exiled Florentine (it was he who broke Michelangelo's nose in a brawl!), who executed it between 1512 and 1518. A few examples of Anglo-Italian sculpture survive from about 1520, like the tomb of John Colet, the English scholar and founder of St Paul's School. These sculpted figures, lying on their sarcophagi, are somewhat provincial versions of the tombs of distinguished scholars in the church of Sta Croce in Florence. Toward the end of the 1510s, Italianate decoration first appeared in England. One of the earliest examples was Cardinal Wolsey's employing of Giovanni da Maiano to execute terracotta busts in roundels in the Grand Entrance of Hampton Court. Italianate surface decoration was referred to as 'antique' or 'Romayne'. One illustration of a royal psalter of about 1540 shows Henry VIII in a chamber with a bed, the foot of which bears a remarkable resemblance to an Italian *cassone* or large chest, often (but not as invariably as once thought) associated with marriage, lion feet and all, and another shows him playing a harp that rests on a *cassone*. However, although bedsteads and various textiles are described as 'Antique', nothing as yet has emerged to prove conclusively that Henry did possess Italian furniture, and it is thought that the artist responsible for the psalter was following conventions that derive from early Italian and French printed books.

Henry VIII strove to emulate Francis I of France, laying on a lavish display at the Field of the Cloth of Gold in Flanders when the two Kings met in 1520, but failed to attract the artists that Francis had. He built an extravagant palace at Nonesuch, near Cheam in Surrey, between 1538 and 1541, doubtless to rival Francis I's achievements and employed among others Nicholas Bellin of Modena, who had actually worked at Fontainebleau. The building was demolished in 1682 but the diarist John Evelyn remarked in 1666 on 'plaster statues and bass-relievos . . . which must needs have been the work of some celebrated Italian'. However, contacts between England and Italy were seriously hampered as a result of the Reformation and the break with the Church of Rome, and very few Italian workmen came.

A few early sixteenth century pieces, such as chairs, survive that are essentially medieval but with classical ornament applied to the surface – a sort of eighteenth-century Gothic revival in reverse! An example is a chair of about 1540 with linenfold decoration and Italianate grotesque putti. The influence is more likely to have come from France or the Netherlands, rather than directly from Italy. Recent researches concerning Flemish workers in England have shown that numbers of woodworkers came to London, mainly to avoid religious persecution. Lists of foreign workers compiled by the Huguenot society show that craftsmen were mainly French, Flemish, Dutch and German rather than Italian, and although London was the main attraction, they settled all over the country. Another example is a slender armchair of about 1530, decorated with female heads and Italianate grotesques, a somewhat cruder version of French chairs of the time, particularly the slender columns. More typical, however, is a folding Glastonbury chair that shows little influence from the new ideas and, other than the rounded arches on the back of the chair, could almost pass as something medieval.

LEFT
Jacques Androuet du Cerceau's design for sea monsters, about 1560. The central motif was incorporated into the Seadog table at Hardwick Hall.

ABOVE RIGHT
Seadog table, English or French, of about 1580, referred to as such in the 1601 inventory of Hardwick Hall.

BELOW RIGHT
Armchair of about 1630 upholstered with 'turkeywork', an English knotted woollen pile, the patterns of which were originally derived from the motifs on Turkish carpets.

By and large it would seem that furniture with the new Italian motifs would have been confined to a select few. Judging from portraits of the time, though that is by no means reliable, Italianate thrones and columned interiors are thought to befit a king, whereas even someone as powerful as Sir Thomas More, posing for Holbein's portrait with his family, is surrounded by furniture that would not have looked out of place in a Netherlandish painting of the 1480s.

King Henry VIII is often regarded as the first English Renaissance king and the furniture listed in the royal inventories would seem to have served to display his wealth and status. The textiles are extravagant, with an abundance of golden fringe or 'Venice Gold' and the royal coats of arms prominently displayed at every opportunity; heraldry is more important than the latest antique design. Terms like 'curiously carved' do not tell us much – they could refer to linenfold or Gothic tracery – but the novelty of Italian-influenced designs might have caught the attention of the inventory compilers. A few royal pieces of the period survive, such as King Henry's writing box, probably by Flemish craftsmen. This was painted and gilt and decorated with a Venus and Mars at either side and trumpet-blowing amorini flanking the royal coat of arms. There are also medallion heads in profile, one of the earliest classical or Romayne motifs to be adopted in England. King Edward VI's leather traveling chest, which was designed to carry documents, was fitted with drawers of leather tooled with geometric patterns and gilt moresques, an intertwining motif that Venice introduced to Europe from the Middle East.

Every schoolboy is taught that the printing press furthered the advance of the new ideas of the Renaissance. It also spread new decorative motifs by way of pattern books. By the late 1540s, French, Flemish and German interpretations of 'grotesque' decoration were spread through various publications by Jacques Androuet du Cerceau, a French architect who flourished between about 1530 and about 1585, Hans Vredeman de Vries (1526-1604?), a Netherlander who seems to have specialized in designing triumphal arches for ceremonial occasions, and Wendel Dietterlin (1551-99) a German mural

painter based mainly in Strasbourg, who was largely responsible for the spread of strapwork, a form of ornament derived from the natural curling of leather skins, at the end of the sixteenth century. The English were also capable of producing works on ornamental design. As early as 1548 Thomas Geminus produced *Morysse and Damashin renewd and encreased Very profitable for Goldsmythes and Embroyderers* and these *morysses* or intertwining patterns found on surviving cups and cushions could easily be adapted for inlay decoration. Christopher Gower intended his *The Waye to Fayre Writing* (London, 1586/7) for among others 'the more ready use and helpe of sundry artificers that work . . . Tymber, Sylk Clothe, Tapestrye, etc'.

The architectural fantasies of Hans Vredeman de Vries, published in *Variae Formae Architecturae* (reprinted in 1601 from a series of earlier engravings made from about 1560 onward) found their way on to monumental cabinets made by German inlayers, the finest examples coming from Augsburg, and on to inlaid chests, erroneously called 'nonesuch chests', in England, which closely re-

semble surviving examples in Cologne and could well have been made in Southwark. 'At St Olaves in Southwark', wrote Edmund Maria Bolton in *Elements of Armorie* (1610), 'You shall learn among the Joyners what *Inlayes and Marquetrie* mean. Inlaye (as the word imports) is a laying of color'd wood in their wainscot works, Bedsteads, Cupbords, Chayres and the like'. A surviving example of the use of inlay on a bedstead is the headboard of the Great Bed of Ware, with panels depicting triumphal arches derived from Vredeman de Vries's *Variae Formae Architectura* and no doubt similar to those he erected for princely ceremonies, such as the entry of Charles V into Antwerp. In addition, Vredeman de Vries published *Differents Pourctraits de Menuiserie* (c. 1588) which included a series of designs for tables, cupboards and state beds. His beds are massive and one incorporated Etruscan sphinxes at the four bottom corners. Those of du Cerceau terminated in rams or eagles with lion's feet; surviving English examples do not quite reach such flights but in the case of the Great Bed of Ware the posts, cornice and headboard offer large surfaces that almost have to be taken up with extravagant decoration. The Great Bed of Ware was doubtless as large as it was to attract more customers, but other examples, less spectacular in scale, are no less ornate; bulbous posts, wainscoted headboards often adorned with coats of arms, testers and soffits are widespread.

Of this group of pieces influenced by northern European pattern books, perhaps the most remarkable survival, and clearly influenced by Jacques Androuet du Cerceau's *Livre des Grottesques* (1566), is the Seadog table at Hardwick Hall. Described as 'a drawing table Carved and guilt standing uppon sea doges inlayde with marble stones and woode' in the 1601 inventory, this rectangular walnut drawer table, so called because it has flaps that can slide out from underneath, rests on four chimeras with dog's heads, bird's wings, women's breasts, seal's fins and fish tails. They in turn rest on a platform held up by four tortoises. The sea monster is derived from a design by du Cerceau, but it cannot be said with certainty whether the table itself is English or French.

As well as the Seadog table, the 1601 inventory of Hardwick Hall, which reflects the tastes of the formidable Bess of Hardwick, one of the richest commoners to move in court circles, also includes carved and gilt cupboards with drawers ('tills') that presumably would have been fitted into the middle shelf, inlaid stools and tables set with marble, and a mother-of-pearl looking glass, in the long gallery. The seating furniture, mostly stools, tends to be covered in velvet, frequently crimson, with elaborate fringes, although other materials such as needlework and silks, are used. The flat surfaces offered by tables and cupboard shelves (not the enclosed type) were covered with carpet. 'A foote turkie carpet' in the Withdrawing Chamber is a rare and early instance of its being used as a floor cover. Perhaps the most sumptuous piece was the state bed in the Pearl Bedchamber, with carved and gilt woodwork surmounted with a tester and double valance, as well as a bedhead of black velvet 'imbrodered with silver golde and pearl'.

Perhaps the greatest Elizabethan architect, Robert Smythson (1536-?1614), left one drawing that approximates to furniture designs which is a *closette*, a library with shelves that diminish the higher they get, and built-in desks and compartments for papers. His son John designed a bed in profile, not one of the massive structures of Vredeman de Vries, but two slender posts like Doric columns, the one at the front shorter, joined at the top by a rod, with an armrest – in fact a frame from which to hang textiles.

The architectural genius of the reigns of James I and Charles I was Inigo Jones, who designed royal masques, a series of allegorical spectacles, as early as 1603. In 1613 he went to Italy in the retinue of the Earl of Arundel and made a thorough study of the architecture of Andrea Palladio of Venice, who was particularly famous for the villas in the country he designed for Venetian patricians and his publication *I Quattro Libri d'Architettura*, (The Four Books of Architecture). Jones managed to purchase Palladio's original drawings as well as those of his pupil Scamozzi. He returned at the end of 1614 to take up the position of Surveyor General, a post he held until 1642, which made him responsible for the building and maintenance of royal properties. He also produced an enormous number of designs for costumes (some highly extravagant) and scenery for masques for both James I and Charles I, spectacles that reinforced the message of the sovereign's benificient rule. His first-hand study of Italian architecture and Roman remains enabled him to produce works in a purely classical style, where the most rigid symmetry, and orders such as Doric, Corinthian and Ionic and the proportions that went with them, triumphed over the mere size and surface decoration of the large Elizabethan edifices. His surviving works include the Queen's House at Greenwich, the Banqueting Hall at Whitehall, and St Pauls, Covent Garden. In addition he worked on a series of interiors in the 1630s for Queen Henrietta Maria that included Somerset House, the Queen's House and Whitehall, borrowing the ideas for fireplaces from French sources like Jean Cotelle, whose drawings helped fill those gaps left by Palladio. Jones's designs for fireplaces make use of Mannerist elements like masks and strapwork but the overall effect is more refined and economical than would have been produced some fifty years

LEFT
The Great Bed of Ware, about 1580. The bed came from the White Hart Inn at Ware in Hertfordshire, and its size made it very much a tourist attraction. The bedhead is decorated with architectural fantasies that derive from Hans Vredeman de Vries.

RIGHT
Court cupboard of about 1620, with a drawer or 'till' for smaller items.

BELOW
Candlestand from Ham House, about 1640; one of a pair, possibly designed by Francis Clein.

earlier. Those close to Charles I, known as the Whitehall Group, willingly adopted this style for decorating their houses, and perhaps the best surviving example is Ham House, the property of William Murray, Earl of Dysart. Elements such as rectangularly partitioned ceilings and doorways similar to Jones's pedimented strapwork chimneypieces appear at Ham. A pair of tables, supported by female caryatids, curve out in a dramatic way, remarkably similar to Jones's design for the monument for Lady Cotton in St Chad's church, Norton-in-Hales, Shropshire. These provide a hint at what furniture designed by Jones could have been like if any of it survived.

Another highly influential designer was Francis Clein, a Dane who had worked for King Christian IV of Denmark, who spent some four years in Italy, and was employed at the Mortlake tapestries from 1625 until 1657. It is likely that he worked at Ham House for Sir William Murray, Earl of Dysart, who acquired the freehold of the property in 1637. The Ham inventory of 1683, compiled in the lifetime of Murray's daughter Elizabeth, states that the insets of the North Drawing Room and ceiling of Mr Murray's closet were painted by Clein, and massive salomonic columns either side of the fireplace in the North Drawing Room are very likely taken from Raphael's cartoons, which were housed at the Mortlake tapestry works. A squab stool (squab being a cushion-cum-mattress) with a pattern possibly done to his design, and a pair of gilt candelabra, are still among the furnishings of Ham House. They have been connected with Clein, and must have seemed avant-garde at the time. Other noteworthy features of Ham of this period are the enormous picture frames executed in the 'auricular' style – a series of curves based on the human ear developed by Friedrich Unteusch, the Frankfurt cabinetmaker who published a series of designs using this motif in his *Neues Zieratenbuch* in about 1645.

Information on the King's furniture is derived from the inventories of Charles I taken during the Commonwealth, and the accounts of the Queen's Robes. The latter provide the names of royal craftsmen such as Philip Broomfield the gilder, Edward Cordell the cabinetmaker, Ralph Grynder the upholsterer, and Charles Goodyeare the joiner. The inventories list what must have been ex-

ABOVE
Spinet known as the Queen Elizabeth Virginals, about 1570, probably from Venice. The decoration includes royal emblems such as Anne Boleyn's raven.

ABOVE
Friedrich Unteusch's design for brackets in the 'auricular style', about 1645.

ABOVE RIGHT
X-frame Chair of State in red velvet in the Leicester Gallery, Knole, about 1660. Although previously thought to have been earlier, a Hampton Court inventory mark and the date 1661 have been found.

BELOW RIGHT
Sgabello chair, a form widespread in Italy in the sixteenth century; this is an English copy of about 1630.

quisite furniture such as 'a rich Cabbonet of Eboney inlayed with silver with flowers and beasts and a clock in the Topp' and 'an ivory cabinet with a paire of Playeing Tables in them, and a looking glasse with sundry empty drawers and An Eight square Table of Ebony inlayed with sundry stones of divers culloures with 4 fete suiteable'. The state bed at Somerset House was 'a large rich French Bedd of sattine richly enbroydered, the outsyde of greene sattine, the inside of white . . .' and matching green satin chairs.

In Charles I's reign a ruling by the London Court of Aldermen in 1632 restricted the carpenters to making benches and cheap tables for '. . . drapers . . . taverners, Victuallers, Chandlers, Compting House Tables and all other Tables made from Deal, Elme, Oake, Beeche or other wood nayled together without glue . . .' and made the joiners responsible for all household furniture from bedsteads to cabinets and fixtures and fittings that involved carving, cutting and the use of glue.

By about 1630 new types of seating had evolved, largely through French and Italian influences, such as the elegant backstool, or what the French called *chaises à vertugadin* (hence the farthingale chair) and the Italian *sgabello*, a heavy and somewhat uncomfortable but nonetheless elegant form seating made from slabs of wood, usually carved into a shell at the back and a mask at the front with a small arch at the bottom and protrusions at the side giving the appearance of feet. One of the earliest recorded appearances of the former in England is in the background of a portrait of the Countess of Arundel in 1617. These chairs were also to be seen at both Ham

House and Holland House, where Francis Clein had worked as a decorator. The farthingale chair (so called in France at any rate because it enabled women to sit in comfort while wearing a farthingale) or backstool, as it would have been called in contemporary English inventories, had an upholstered back rest and seat but the legs and uprights tended to be in the form of slender Doric columns. Curiously, far fewer of these elegant pieces have survived than the massive, ornately carved and inlaid armchairs of oak that continued to be made well into the last decades of the seventeenth century.

By about 1600 the large tables of the great halls were generally used by servants. The house owner ate more frequently in the privacy of his parlor and bed chamber, hence the need for a smaller table or one that could be folded away when not needed. If he was going to dine in the hall, something he hardly ever did after the English Civil War (the dining hall became the reserve of the servants, who were being gradually pushed out of sight after the Restoration) he and the steward tended to use drawer tables, which were fitted with drawleaves, that would slide out and expand the table surface when necessary. These pieces could be fairly substantial and the Duke of Somerset's 1552 inventory mentions 'two long drawing tables of Walnuttree'. This is borne out by surviving examples of the late sixteenth century. These pieces tended to have bulbous legs, often surmounted with Ionic capitals, or straight ones surmounted with the Doric order. It has been customary to date the former type earlier, but whereas Hans Vredeman de Vries used the latter in his designs, his son Paul included ones with

ABOVE
Armchair with inlaid decoration, about 1670, possibly from Yorkshire. This massive, provincial form has various classical ornaments such as consoles and balustrading, and the arms curve downwards in the contemporary fashion.

LEFT
Draw table, about 1610. Note the flaps underneath the top which can be pulled out, expanding the surface.

bulbous Ionic legs in his publication *Versheyden Schrynwerk* (Amsterdam, 1630) some forty years later, which suggests that there was no simple progression from Doric to Ionic.

All tables the size of drawer tables or smaller would have been covered by a carpet (they only start being laid on the floor in about 1600, being described in the Hardwick inventory as 'foote carpets') and the large tables in the hall would have been covered with coarse linen, the legs hidden and not an important feature, subject to the changes of fashion. It is interesting to compare tables of the 1654 inventory of Ham House with those of the 1670s; the earlier ones are listed with carpets and the later ones with protective covers of leather, or decorative ones of materials like sarsnet or paragon (sarsnet being a type of silk and paragon a worsted material). Folding tables had been used since the Middle Ages and by the mid seventeenth century an even more effective space-saver was introduced, in the form of the gateleg table. Its hinged flaps and swinging legs meant that it could be placed out of the way against a wall.

BELOW
Lacquer cabinet, probably English and owing more to Venetian-cum-Islamic than Far Eastern ornament, of about 1630.

ABOVE
The Knole Settee in the Leicester Gallery, Knole, about 1660. Previously dated to about 1610, this ancestor of the modern sofa is very similar to a description of a 'large Couch of green damaske' made for the Royal Household by John Casbert in about 1661.

RIGHT
'Standing bed', of about 1580, formerly from Moreton Corbet Castle, Shropshire.

The role of the 'cupboard' or 'court cupboard' requires some explanation; toward the end of the sixteenth century it took on a meaning similar to that it has today. A large structure with doors, used for storage, was known as a 'press' as late as 1672. In the Hardwick inventory these cupboards could have tills or drawers, presumably fitted into the table (or shelf if there was more than one tier). By 1600 'livery cupboardes' like the one at Ingateston had 'a bottom and two close cupboards with lockes and keyes' – so presumably they were closed. The term 'liveries' meant rations of food and so their main use was to store food, wine or ale. They were often placed in bed chambers should one feel hungry or thirsty at night and provided a useful surface on which to put candles and other bits and pieces by the bedside.

In the seventeenth century cabinets appeared. Unlike the chest, they were not used for storing plate or food but were divided into small square drawers, into which documents, curios and even jewelry were kept. The use of lavish materials such as ebony, ivory and tortoiseshell and cunning arrangements of drawers to allow for secret compartments indicate the status and privacy of these pieces. The Ham House inventory of 1655 mentions 'one black ebonie cabinet', and this could well refer to one such piece. As to their origin, the Spanish *vargueño*, an early form of cabinet on a stand, and Japanese lacquer cabinets seem most likely. The most prized cabinets were made in Antwerp, part of the Spanish Netherlands, and the arrangement of drawers is similar enough, although the doors of Antwerp cabinets opened outward and the single door of the *vargueño* dropped downwards, like the scriptoir, the ancestor of the bureau. More direct contact with the Far East, made possible by the navigational feats of the Portuguese at the end of the fifteenth century and encouraged by the expanding spice trade, resulted in more Chinese and Japanese goods, including lacquer cabinets, appearing in Europe towards the end of the sixteenth century. In 1614 the Earl of Northampton was recorded as owning a 'china guilt cabonette upon a frame'. In the inventories of Charles I quite a number of 'india cabinets' feature and Edward Cordell described himself as 'Her Majesty's (Henrietta Maria's) cabinet maker'.

Surviving beds of the late sixteenth century are often described as 'standing beds' and the 1605 Marton inventory refers to one 'with a waneskot tester'. Although they were massive and lavishly decorated, few survive. The most prestigious examples, like their medieval counterparts, served as vehicles for elaborate textiles. Posts supported the tester, a roof-like structure, from which curtains hung. The most common arrangement was for the curtains to move horizontally along the tester and for the rods to be masked by valances. By the late sixteenth century 'French Beds', simple, textile-covered box-like structures, were introduced. Sir Henry Unton had three French Beds, but then he had been ambassador to France. The term 'French Bed' recurs in Charles I's inventory. A simple form was the 'couch bed', which had posts at the corners and a headboard for stability. Charles I had one such 'couch beddstead, the head posts, post(s) and feete thereof richly guilte'. Servants' beds were usually tucked away in odd corners, like the landing outside the Countess of Shrewsbury's rooms at Hardwick in the form of 'a bedsted to turne up like a chest'. There was a settle bedstead at Harte Hall, and the porter at Ham House slept by the front door on 'one presse bed of walnutree'.

Inigo Jones, denied royal patronage following the death of Charles I, died in obscurity but architectural innovations still took place. Sir Roger Pratt built Coleshill for his cousin Sir George Pratt, a four-storey house in the style of Jones with a strictly symmetrically planned interior and exterior, the latter of plain ashlar. John Webb created the first portico with giant orders – it ascended three storeys – at The Vyne and Philip, 4th Earl of Pembroke the magnificent Baroque double-cubed room at Wilton. The Commonwealth is regarded as a drab and philistine period but the nation prospered and, as far as is known, joiners and upholsterers were by no means reduced to penury. Furthermore, the 1655 inventory of Ham House shows that wealth continued to be displayed. However, the return of the monarchy was to herald great advances that brought international prominence to English cabinetmakers.

CHAPTER 3

The Later Stuarts

English Baroque

THE RETURN of Charles II from exile in 1660 and the restoration of the English monarchy brought about a flowering of architecture and decorative arts. The rebuilding of St Paul's, for example, included Grinling Gibbons's monumental and ornately carved choir stalls and bishop's throne. One of Gibbons's earliest royal commissions was to provide the exquisite carving for Hugh May's decoration of Windsor Castle. The return of the Court and the royal patronage that went with it, as well as ambitious building programmes, played their part in raising standards of English craftsmanship, particularly carving and cabinetmaking, to new heights. A second boost was provided by the influx of French Huguenot craftsmen following the revocation of the Edict of Nantes by Louis XIV in 1685 and the resulting persecution of Protestants in that country. The Glorious Revolution of 1688 and William of Orange's arrival made England an even safer refuge. The published designs of William's architect, Daniel Marot, himself an exiled French Protestant, were to have a profound effect on English interior decoration, particularly in the form of his flamboyant state beds.

To summarize the development of style during this period, furniture from about 1660 until 1690 remained essentially rectilinear, with an abundance of surface decoration wherever the opportunity arose. Cabinets were set on stands with columns, usually Doric, salomonic or in some form of term, joined by stretchers above the ball-feet. The same is the case with tables. However, the stands which supported lacquer cabinets were usually gilt and often curvaceous, sometimes in the form of foliate scrolls or, in the case of an example at Ham House, elephant's trunks. The legs of such stands were often joined by floral swags with putti at the top, as well as curved stretchers at the bottom. Chairs were often set on turned legs joined with stretchers whose design often repeated the crest at the back, particularly in the high wicker chair backs of William III's reign. Upholstered chairs were provided with square back-rests and supports separating them from the seats. By the eighteenth century these supports had disappeared altogether and the back was joined to the seat. The great innovation in design was the cabriole leg. This curved device, strengthened at the top, could support the seat, thus rendering stretchers obsolete. The seat and back broadened and became more curvaceous and the feet took on a greater variety of design, with the Italianate lion's paw making its appearance.

The most sought-after wood for cabinetmaking was French walnut, although supplies were seriously affected by the hard winter of 1709. Tropical woods such as kingwood and amboyna were used for inlay, and ebony was preferred for prestigious pieces like looking glasses and cabinets of curiosities. Mahogany, which was to dominate in the next century, made isolated appearances such

LEFT
Joined armchair of mahogany, 1661, from Trinity Hall, Aberdeen, one of the earliest examples of the use of mahogany.

ABOVE
Marquetry table, about 1675, part of the original furnishings of Ham House.

as the Flesher's company chair from Trinity Hall, Aberdeen, dated 1661. As early as 1672, Richard Blome wrote in his *Description of Jamaica*, 'Here are a great variety of woods . . . Red wood, a kind of Logg-wood, etc., also Cedar, Mothogeney'.

In this period, the cabinetmaker's skill came to the fore, as John Evelyn noted in his *Whole Body of Ancient and Modern Architecture* (1680). Walnut was the most fashionable wood for veneer or joinery. Inlay and marquetry, which had been used in the previous century by German craftsmen to depict architectural fantasies, were brought to high levels on cabinets and tables by craftsmen like

Gerrit Jensen and Cornelius Golle. Inlay involved cutting in to the surface, while marquetry was a covering of different colored woods and ivory to go hand in hand with veneer. From the 1660s onward the main decoration was in arabesques, nicknamed 'seaweed', or floral, influenced by Dutch flower paintings, in which flowers were depicted sprouting from a pot rather than in a garland or swag.

Furniture of a more specialist nature appeared, such as the drop-front scriptor, whose many compartments could hide sensitive documents and whose cover came down and rested on slats of wood that slid out from the stand, thus providing a flat, stable surface on which to write. Cabinets could be used for storing collections and curiosities. The elaborate decoration, often in marquetry or inlay of kingwood and amboyna with silver mounts, such as those at Ham House, indicates what precious pieces they were. Books had been stored on shelves, and in a few instances miniature versions were placed in cases, also fitted with shelves and serving as portable

ABOVE
Lacquer cabinet on a highly ornate Baroque stand. The laquer is probably either Dutch or English.

BELOW
Sleeping chair at Ham House, about 1679; the back is adjustable, and the back legs rake outward.

libraries. In 1666 Pepys had special bookcases with glazed doors made for him by a joiner called Sympson, the first of their kind. Gateleg tables continued to replace the massive draw tables, and tea tables, mostly imported from the Far East until the beginning of the next century, made their appearance, as the new, fashionable and highly expensive drink became known in England.

Expanding trade with the Far East resulted in the widespread use of lacquer cabinets, screens, tables and even tea trays for furnishing the apartments of courtiers and houses of merchants. On 30th July 1682, John Evelyn 'went over to visit our good neighbour Mr Boon, whose whole house is a cabinet (here meaning closet, or small room adjoining a bedroom, *cabinet* in French) of elegancies, especially Indian, and the contrivement of the Japan skreenes instead of wainscott in the Hall. . . .' – so a whole room was made of lacquer. Not only could oddments be stored in cabinets but Chinese porcelain could be placed both on top and underneath – a habit that Queen Mary made fashionable, much to the anger of that inveterate xenophobe Daniel Defoe.

In every country in Christendom lacquer cabinets were fashionable but expensive and the joinery of oriental furniture left a lot to be desired. Captain William Dampier complained 'the joyners in this Country may not compare their work with that the Europeans make'. So although William Whitewood was being a little optimistic when he claimed in 1683 'English varnished cabinets may vie with the oriental', there were plenty of opportunities for English cabinetmakers to provide better constructed pieces, albeit with coarser imitation lacquer.

John Stalker and George Parker published a very detailed *Treatise of Japanning, Varnishing and Gilding* (1688) for those trying to produce imitations of the Japanese originals, whether professionals, or amateurs like the daughter of a certain Edmund Verney who wrote to her in 1689 'I find you have a desire to learn Jappan, as you call it, and I approve it; . . . for I admire all accomplishments that will render you considerable and Lovely in the sight of God and man . . .' By now japaning was becoming a genteel, ladylike pastime, presumably when applied to a screen, tray or anything that did not require complicated joinery.

Chairs were now more generously upholstered. Easy chairs were fully padded on all the surfaces. Horse hair was considered a good form of padding, regarded as hygienic and easier to keep in place than other materials. The top of armrests were covered with padding until about 1670, after which they tended to curve and lose their covering. The backs of what were called 'French chairs' were curved (or 'hollow' or 'crooked') to accommodate the sitter. Although chairs became more com-

LEFT

Scriptor with silver handles and escutcheons and kingwood 'oysterwork' veneer, about 1675, part of the original furnishings of Ham House.

RIGHT

Bookcase from the Pepys Library, Magdalene College, Cambridge, part of a set of twelve, 1666, formerly belonging to Samuel Pepys and among the earliest with glass fronts.

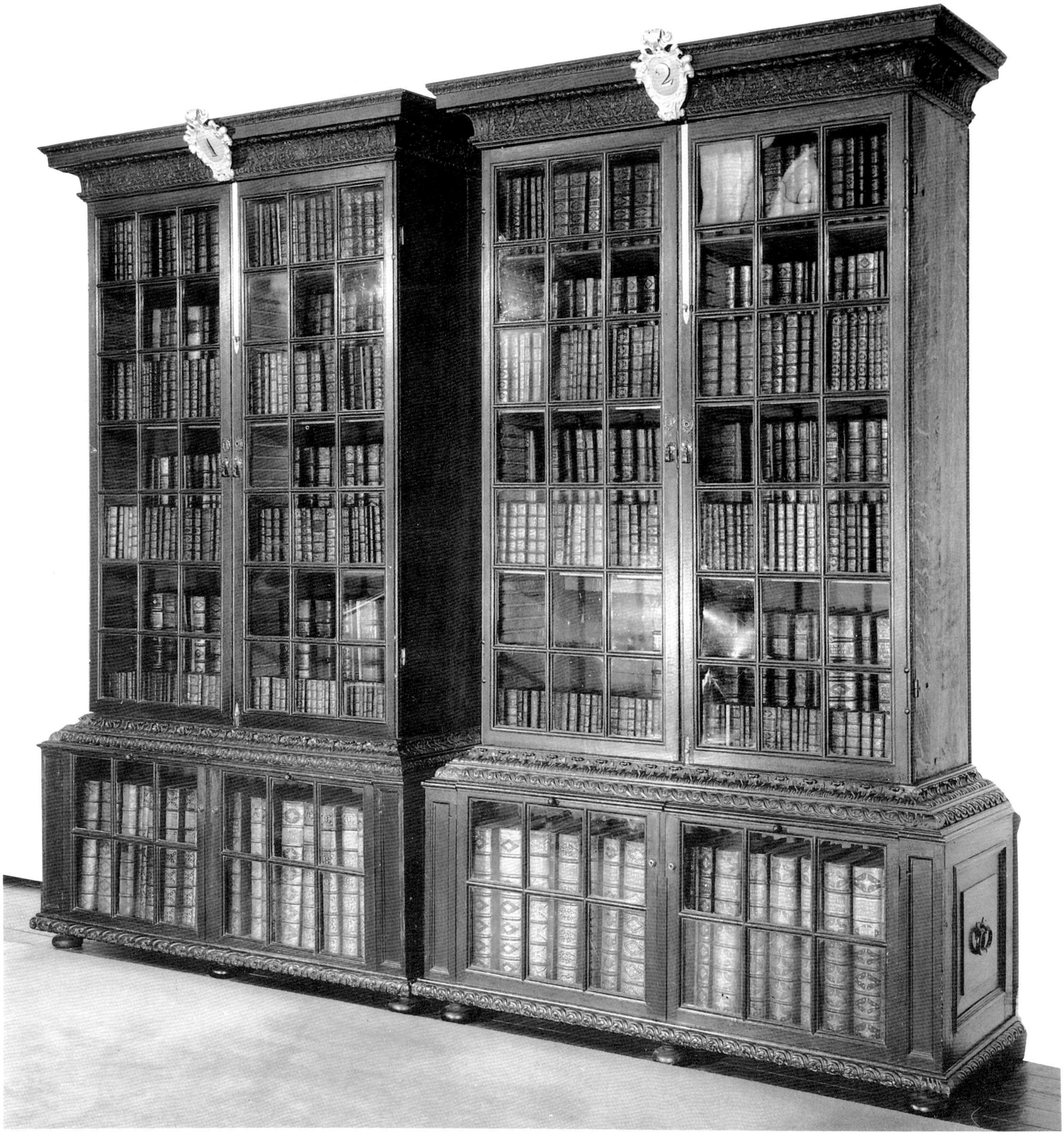

fortable as the seventeenth century continued, the emphasis was on show and the dignity of the owner and much attention was paid to details such as elaborate fringes, which could greatly enhance the visual effect without making the chair any more agreeable to sit on! Chairs with more expensive materials often had protective covers, those of Ham House being sarsnet or paragon (sarsnet being a type of silk and paragon a tough worsted form of wool).

The sleeping chair, with an adjustable back and closed in at the side to exclude daylight and induce sleep, became fashionable. John Evelyn had come across them in Rome in 1644. Richard Pryce designed a sleeping chair 'to fall in the back – of irone worke' in 1675 and John Paudevin supplied a number for Catherine of Braganza two years later. It has been suggested that he also made the surviving examples at Ham House, owing to the Duke of Lauderdale's intimacy with the Court. These chairs could be adjusted by means of iron quadrants and holes with gilt pegs, and the back legs were raked backwards for greater stability. Another luxurious item of which quite a few examples survive is the daybed. One of the finest was made by Philip Guibert in about 1700 for the Duke of Leeds at Temple Newsham. He also made 'a fine black

soffa of a new fashion, filled up with downe, the frieze and cheeks all molded and fringed' for William III in 1697. Sofas and daybeds served as excellent show-off pieces for upholsterers.

Payments survive for upholstery work for King Charles II from his restoration onward, even if we cannot be sure if his pieces survive. John Casbert provided seating and canopies of estate for Whitehall, Windsor Castle and Somerset House. An animated petition survives from Robert Morris for the year 1661 for his account to be settled, following the supply of extensive furnishing for the King and Queen Mother and seventy-five chairs of turkeywork for the House of Commons – a bill of 'nine thousand Eight hundred odd pounds' of which only six hundred had been paid. Turkeywork was a widely used woolen form of upholstery, developed in England in the sixteenth century in imitation of Turkish carpets. Woolen materials such as serge were used for cheaper chair covers. Silken materials used were often brocades, but gold and silver thread were used less for chair upholstery in the seventeenth century, as they were thought to be scratchy. Genoa velvets were little used until the end of the seventeenth century, a fine example being the Duke of Leeds' sleeping chair and sofa.

The simple innovation of cane-seating, introduced to England in 1664, proved to be more comfortable than what had gone before, and chairs of this type remained popular well into the eighteenth century. In 1680 the Cane-Chair Makers Company were able to claim that their products were liked for 'their durability, lightness, and cleanness from Dust, Worms and Moths which inseparably attend Turkey-work, serge and other stuff chairs and couches, to the spoiling of them and all furniture near them'. They also claimed that cane chairs were exported 'into almost all parts of the world where heat renders turkeywork useless'. At Ham House, the rare instance of a cane table and *torchères* survive. Although these particular examples could be Dutch – the Duchess of Lauderdale paid a Mistress Van der Huva 440 gilders for a 'cabinet of black ebonie with a table and two Gadons (*guéridons*)' which could be them – Thomas Roberts, the royal upholsterer, left a bill for 'a fine cane table, wrought hand-

LEFT
Daybed and sofa upholstered with Genoese silk, about 1700, originally supplied by Philip Guibert to the Duke of Leeds' house at Kiverton, Yorks.

RIGHT
Triad (looking glass, two stands and table) from Ham House, probably Dutch and supplied to the Duchess of Lauderdale by Mistress Van Huva in 1672. A rare surviving example of cane being used for tabletops, such as both Dutch and English joiners were supplying at the time.

BELOW
Backstool covered with turkeywork, about 1650.

RIGHT
Squab stool, about 1640, covered with what might be Mortlake tapestry and designed by Francis Clein. Oriental style lacquer decoration is just visible on the ball feet.

some with a scrolled frame and scrolled pillars' in 1691.

Before Galileo Galilei observed the regular swing of the pendulum, and his son Vicenzo turned his discoveries to practical use by setting up a pendulum clock in Venice in 1649, domestic clocks, usually set in ornate metal cases, were driven by a tense coiled spring unwinding and large ones (for clock towers) by a series of weights rising and falling at a controled speed. The Dutch mathematician Christian Van Zulichem brought Vicenzo Galilei's pendulum clock to prominence in Holland, and his friend Ahasuerus Fromanteel introduced it to England in 1658. Dr Robert Hooke developed a heavy pendulum that could swing for a long time in small arcs, and his innovations and those of William Clement made the development of the long-case clock possible.

One of the greatest cabinetmakers of the period was Gerrit Jensen (fl. 1680-d. 1715), a man of obscure but probably Netherlandish origins, and he was heavily influenced by Pierre Golle, the eminent cabinetmaker to

LEFT
Japaned chair about 1675 with caned seat, the back as lavishly decorated as the front. Part of the original furnishings of Ham House.

NEAR RIGHT
Long case clock, about 1660, by Ahasuerus Fromanteel, who is credited with introducing the pendulum-operated clock to England.

FAR RIGHT ABOVE
Set of silver furniture made for the 6th Earl of Dorset by Gerrit Jensen in 1680.

FAR RIGHT BELOW
Stool from the King's Room, Knole, covered in silver and gold brocade, about 1670.

Louis XIV of France and a specialist in inlay. Jensen provided a particularly fine arabesque or 'seaweed' marquetry writing table for Queen Mary at Kensington Palace in 1690 and an inlaid walnut mirror for James II at Windsor Castle in 1686. His activity spanned from 1680, when he is recorded as making a set of furniture for the King of Morocco, until his death in 1715. As well as the king, his patrons included nobles such as the 'Proud' Duke of Somerset and the Earl of Dorset. There are records of his working as far afield as Hamilton Palace, Lanarkshire, as well as Boughton, Petworth and Knole, where his famous suite of silver furniture survives. Oak frames are covered with highly ornate silver embossed mostly with acanthus. The table top has a large oval plaque in the middle depicting the competition between Marsyas and Apollo and the legs curve in an S-scroll joined by concave stretchers, characteristic of grand tables of the 1670s. The stands terminate in a tripod of S-curved brackets, as is characteristic of the baroque *torchère*. The whole ensemble or triad must have looked spectacular when illuminated with flicker-

LEFT *State bed from the King's Room, Knole, about 1670, probably French; the hangings are silver and gold brocade. The seating and the bed have been attributed to Jean Peyrard, Louis XIV's upholsterer, who supplied furniture to Charles II between 1672 and 1673.*

ABOVE *Marquetry cabinet on stand, about 1680, part of the original furnishings of Ham House.*

ing candles. Other documented pieces by Jensen to survive include a glass-fronted cabinet and marquetry table at Kensington Palace, a pier glass with a royal cypher and crown in blue glass at Hampton Court, a pair of *verre églomisé* glasses for the Duke of Somerset at Petworth and a fine pair of metal inlaid cabinets at Boughton.

Jensen's great contemporary was Thomas Roberts (d. 1714), of The Royal Chair, Marylebone St, London who specialized in providing seating, state beds and screens. (His son Richard provided new lions for St Edward's Throne in Westminster Abbey). His clients included James II and the Duke of Devonshire and his style showed an abundance of putti and flowers, carved in fine detail. His most famous piece to survive is the state bed with matching chairs and stools for James II, made shortly before James fled to France and currently in the Venetian ambassador's room at Knole, which the Earl of Dorset claimed as a perquisite. Hung in blue-green Genoa velvet, it has a flamboyantly carved tester that includes the crown, royal monogram, lion and unicorn and amorini, and flares outward according to fashions from the mid 1680s onwards. He also made Queen Anne's Coronation Throne, now at Hatfield.

The interiors of Charles Le Brun, the architect responsible for the *Grand Galerie* at Versailles and Vaux-le-Vicomte, the palace Louis XIV seized from his disgraced finance minister Fouquet, aimed at external and internal unity, its furniture playing an important part in the overall scheme. However, there is less evidence of this being the case in England. Perhaps it is partly an accident of survival, as very few designs of furniture survive until Daniel Marot visited England in 1689. Exceptions include John Talman's design for a cabinet of curiosities of about 1700

LEFT
Headboard of the state bed which belonged to the Earl of Melville, made for his residence, Melville House, Fife. The flamboyant design shows the influence of Daniel Marot.

BELOW
Tea table, Javanese(?) top with English additions in the lower part. Tea was a very fashionable and expensive drink in England, and this is an example of the furniture that went with it. This was certainly at Ham in 1683. Repairs of 1730 mention the providing of a frame, which looks, however, to date to about 1675.

RIGHT
Lacquer cabinet on gilt stand, about 1690. The japanning is English and shows the influence of Stalker and Parker's A Treatise in Japanning and Lacquering (1688).

and John Webb's bedchamber at Greenwich of 1665. Talman's cabinet is set on a flamboyant baroque stand, and flanked by stools of a similar design. Webb's state bed is a 'French bed' and very much a simple rectilinear structure, surmounted with ostrich feathers at the four corners.

Daniel Marot (c. 1663-1752), a pupil of Jean Le Pautre, was forced into exile following the revocation of the Edict of Nantes and found employment as architect to William of Orange, later William III of England. His work at Hampton Court is recorded as being mostly concerned with the layout of the garden, but one collection of engravings has the title *New Book of Furnishings Designed and Engraved by D. Marot, Architect to his British Majesty*. Included is an engraving of a bedchamber where the state bed, with flamboyant half tester and headboard, is flanked by matching chairs neatly arranged against the wall. His designs were highly influential among upholsterers like François Lapierre. Marot's version of the state bed was far more elaborate than the simple, rectilinear French bed; he added a highly flamboyant, flared tester, in his new Protestant environment. Lapierre's tester for the Melville

state bed, although four poster, used elaborately scrolled carving that projects beyond the strictly rectangular confines of the French bed. The beds that Marot designed tended to be half-tester; the canopy only covered half the bed. When Celia Fiennes visited the Duke of Norfolk's apartment at Windsor Castle, she noticed a 'half bedstead as the new mode'. Contemporary accounts of the highly ornate bed that Thomas Roberts made for the Great Bed Chamber at Windsor show evidence of strong influence by Daniel Marot. They refer to 'a large moulding oval Tester and headboard, and ironworks to support the tester and cornices' as well as 'rich carved work' on the tester. Included in Marot's designs are chairs, stools and tables with the new cabriole leg and S-shaped structure, probably derived from Far Eastern furniture, which was to dominate English furniture until the 1760s and the introduction of which is usually, rightly or wrongly, identified with the reign of Queen Anne.

At the beginning of the eighteenth century, England enjoyed increasing prosperity. The increase of cabinet-

makers in the 1690s, half of them with English names, indicates that cabinetmaking was being taken up by native workers and was being seen as a worthwhile trade with an expanding market. Improvements in the making of sprung carriages made London more accessible and the shops of upholsterers and cabinetmakers were more enticing than anything the carpenter on the estate might cobble together. The Duke of Montrose furnished his lodgings in Glasgow with furniture ordered from John Gumley, and John Mellor of Erddig bought extensively from both Gumley and John Belchier. Outstanding craftsmen like Gumley (fl. 1691-1727) and James Moore Sr (1670-1726) emerged. Gumley specialized in the manufacture of plate glass, but his firm provided furniture of all kinds for Hampton Court, Chatsworth and Erddig. Surviving examples are usually bordered with glass with giltwood edges, and surmounted with flamboyantly outlined crests often decorated with coats of arms. Although desks and bureaux from his workshop survive, his extant pieces are predominantly looking-glasses, as one would expect from someone who called his premises The Glass Gallery. When he died in 1727 he left a substantial fortune and William Pulteney, later Lord Bath, married his daughter. Alexander Pope's satirical poem *The Looking-Glass* included the verse:

> Could the sire renowned in
> Glass produce
> One faithful mirror for his
> Daughter's use?

James Moore Sr, who formed a partnership with Gumley, is famous for his gilt-gesso furniture. Gesso or plaster of paris would be applied to the wooden surface, stamped with decorative patterns while still wet, and sprinkled with sand to create a granulated effect. When it had dried, a linseed-oil based mordant would then be applied and the gold leaf added while the surface was still tacky. This furniture consisted mostly of sidetables and stands, such as those that have survived at Kensington Palace bearing the cypher of George I and stamped 'Moore'. Other examples are various stands decorated with the Grecian key-pattern, and possibly a chest from Shobden Court which bears the crest of William Bateman, later Viscount Bateman, who married a granddaughter of Sarah, Duchess of Marlborough. This gilt marriage chest is loosely based on the Italian *cassone*, although with an abundance of baroque scroll ornament.

LEFT
Wassail set, about 1675, consisting of a table, two candlestands, two candlesticks, a wassail bowl and lidded spice dish and four dipper cups. The term 'Wassail' is an Anglo-Saxon toast meaning 'good health'.

RIGHT
French bureau of brass and marquetry pewter, by Pierre Golle, said to have been presented to Ralph, 1st Duke of Montagu, by Louis XIV. Gerrit Jensen also provided a metal inlaid chest of drawers for Montagu. Golle's son Cornelius made furniture for Queen Mary.

BELOW
Cravat of limewood, carved by Grinling Gibbons in about 1680 in imitation of Venetian point lace, and at one time the property of Horace Walpole.

James Moore is also recorded as having provided furniture for the Duke of Buccleuch at Dalkieth Palace, Scotland, North Cray, Lincolnshire and Marlborough House. His good working relationship with Sarah, Duchess of Marlborough, who referred to him as her 'oracle', meant that he took over the building of Blenheim following the dismissal of Vanbrugh. Other important cabinetmakers included John Belchier, who supplied furniture for Erddig, and the prolific firm of John Cox and G. Coxed & T. Woster. Belchier's state bed for Erddig survives, with a pair of gilt girandoles and a glass-topped table with the Mellor coat of arms. A large number of desks, bureaus, secretaires and chests of drawers of the period survive, bearing the trade labels of Coxed and Woster. They frequently incorporated looking-glasses in their bureaus and embellished them with kingwood, crossbanding and pewter, and pieces such as these made their way as far afield as Williamsburg, Virginia.

After the Restoration of the monarchy, therefore, English furniture rose from its provincial backwater to international importance. This was largely brought about by foreign designers such as Marot and cabinetmakers such as Jensen, carvers like Grinling Gibbons, and a court that aimed at the splendor of Louis XIV, even if absolutism was not politically expedient nor money always forthcoming. This love of splendor was in no way diminished by the succession of William of Orange, with Daniel Marot in his retinue. By 1715 Elizabeth Charlotte d'Orleans was forced to concede 'one can no longer send such fashions because the English have their own, which are followed here now'.

CHAPTER 4

Early Georgian

Palladian and Rococo

FOR ABOUT the first forty years of Hanoverian rule the two most powerful influences on English taste were William Kent, the foremost Palladian architect and interior decorator, on the one hand, and St Martin's Academy, the main propagator of the Rococo style, on the other. In this century, architecture increasingly influenced furniture styles; William Kent, Henry Flitcroft and others made the pieces an integral part of the design of the interior. At the same time the upholsterer and cabinetmaker began to assert themselves. Francis Croxford, for instance, was 'eminent in his profession for his many new and beautiful designs' and Elijan Chupain and Thomas Van Hausen produced 'many new and beautiful designs the cabinet way'. Others went so far as to publish large collections of designs, solely of furniture, as was the case with Thomas Chippendale and Ince and Mayhew.

Even if Palladian architecture prevailed during the reigns of the first two Georges, the architect had to accept the fact that the client, or at any rate his wife, would often want the latest fashions in furniture and upholstery, and from the 1730s onward these were French Rococo. Any designer would have to include furniture with an abundance of S-scrolls and *rocaille* motifs in his published collections of designs if they were to sell and this made them remarkably eclectic in their styles, making use of Gothic, Rococo, Palladian and Chinoiserie motifs.

One of the main problems in following the architectural style of Andrea Palladio and Inigo Jones was that these architects left behind no easily identifiable furniture designs, with the possible exception of the rather uncomfortable *sgabello*-type hall chair. The idea of James Moore Sr's marriage chest, based on the Italian *cassone*, did not take root with Lord Burlington and William Kent, even though it was probably more similar to the furniture that would have been found in Palladio's interiors than the massive architectural furniture of Kent. Where a

LEFT

Sidetable from Spenser House designed by John Vardy in about 1750. The decoration with Bacchic motifs, such as vine shoots and grapes, panthers and the mask of the god of wine, would suggest that this originally belonged to the Eating Room.

LEFT
Pierglass and table of about 1745 by Mathias Lock for the Drawing Room of Hinton House, Somerset, the residence of the 2nd Earl Paulett.

ABOVE
Gilt sidetable, about 1730, designed by William Kent for Chiswick House, the villa of Lord Burlington.

RIGHT
Portrait of Grace Carteret, 4th Countess of Dysart, by John Vanderbrank about 1735; note the table leg with a female term, similar to designs by Nicholas Pineau and Batty Langley.

furniture style was lacking, it had to be invented and the most logical place from which to borrow it was from richly moulded door architraves, large pediments, consoles and sculpture. Even if Kent did design a petticoat depicting the five orders for a lady, this furniture was both monumental and rather heavy, unlike Rococo.

John Vardy, an architect very much of the Kentian mould, was only too happy to produce a lighter and more florid version of Kent – his drawing of a royal bed, dated 1749, is the Houghton bed, originally with a heavily moulded classical tester, but this time very much à la Rococo. The purist might admire the external architecture of Palladio, and advocate its use for monumental, pedimeted fireplaces, but the lighter Rococo ornament, particularly when applied to pier glasses, pier tables, seating and beds, tended to dominate inside, when show was called for. Furniture in contemporary conversation pieces was often rather plain and understated and more suitable for private surroundings. One of the characters in George Colman's *The Clandestine Marriage* said in mockery of Rococo, 'Ay, here's none of your straight lines here – but all taste – zig-zag – crinkum-crankum – in and out –

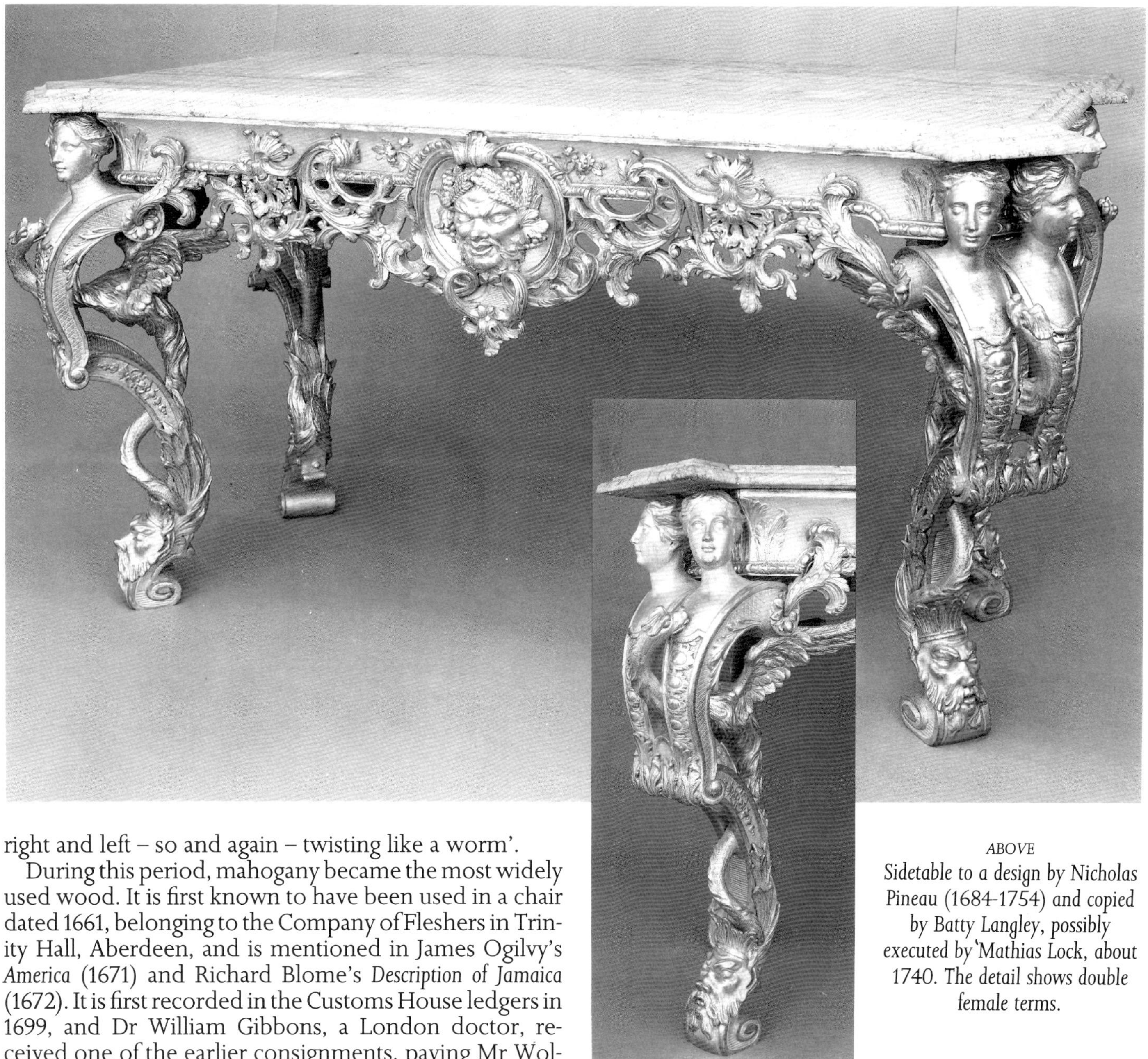

ABOVE
Sidetable to a design by Nicholas Pineau (1684-1754) and copied by Batty Langley, possibly executed by 'Mathias Lock, about 1740. The detail shows double female terms.

right and left – so and again – twisting like a worm'.

During this period, mahogany became the most widely used wood. It is first known to have been used in a chair dated 1661, belonging to the Company of Fleshers in Trinity Hall, Aberdeen, and is mentioned in James Ogilvy's *America* (1671) and Richard Blome's *Description of Jamaica* (1672). It is first recorded in the Customs House ledgers in 1699, and Dr William Gibbons, a London doctor, received one of the earlier consignments, paying Mr Wollaston, a cabinetmaker of Longacre, to make a candle box and later a bureau from this wood. Sir Robert Walpole not only exempted Jamaican mahogany from import duty, making it cheaper than the more sought after Cuban or 'Spanish' mahogany, but also had the staircases and paneling of Houghton Hall made in this material. James Richards, the carver and joiner, executed the work.

Mahogany was popular with cabinetmakers as it enabled crisp, high-quality carving, it was stable and resistant to warping and woodworm, and came in large planks, making it suitable for all kinds of furniture. Walnut still had its devotees in the earlier decades of the century, but by 1776 Dr Hunter was writing in his edition of John Evelyn's *Silva*, 'Formerly the walnut tree was much propagated for its wood, but since the importation of mahogany and Virginia walnut it has considerably decreased in reputation'. Native woods such as elm, oak and beech were often used, as is evident in the large number of 'Windsor' chairs, many of which were made in High Wycombe, owing to the abundance of beech there. In the 1720s marble-top tables became more widespread, although one was supplied to the Duke of Lauderdale at Ham House as early as the 1670s. Under Italian influences, brought about by the Grand Tour, this material became more fashionable, with Mathew Brettingham the Younger despatching seven cases containing marbles in 1764. At Badminton, Dr Pococke noticed several tables, 'Some of Alabastro Fiorentino, one or two of Porphyry'.

In the first decade of the eighteenth century the cabriole leg replaced the straightened version on chairs, tables and stands. No doubt the variety of feet with which they could terminate, ranging from lion's paws to claw-and-balls, did much to enhance their popularity. This structure was remarkably stable and by about 1720, if not earlier, it became apparent that stretchers near the feet were no longer necessary. Bracket feet, curved on the inside, replaced the bun feet characteristic of the late seventeenth century, underneath chests of drawers, bookcases and bureau cabinets. Seventeenth century scriptors had stood on stands reinforced with stretchers, but as the eighteenth century progressed increasing numbers of bureaus rested on chests of drawers with bracket feet. However, a number of earlier examples rested on stands

LEFT Pierglass and sidetable with a glass top, 1723-26, bearing the Mellor coat of arms, supplied by John Belchier, a fashionable cabinetmaker, to John Mellor at Erddig, N. Wales.

RIGHT State bed at Houghton, the country residence of Sir Robert Walpole, designed by William Kent about 1730. Following Walpole's fall from office in 1742 most of the bills, including that for the state bed, were destroyed. However, the gold trimmings alone, supplied by Turner, Hill and Pitter of the Strand, cost £1,219 3s 11d.

ABOVE Sketch of a piertable and an account, about 1745, by Mathias Lock, concerning work in the Tapestry Room at Hinton House, Somerset.

with cabriole legs, an echo of the old practice. During the early eighteenth century the kneehole desk developed, with narrow drawers at either side, thus accommodating the sitter more comfortably. Whereas the scriptor and cabinet of curiosities largely followed the arrangement of the Japanese lacquered imports, the bureau and desk provided pigeonholes, small rectangular drawers and recesses from which the sitter could take papers as he needed them. Chests of drawers, or chests on chests, developed from the massive presses and proved a useful and, given the attention they received from cabinetmakers, an attractive method of storage, which enhanced the bedchamber as well as the closet. Looking-glasses, such as were made by John Belchier and John Gumley, became more elongated in design as techniques improved. As toilet mirrors they were set on small carcases with drawers, and as large, grand and usually gilt pier-glasses they stood between windows, above sidetables and behind candle-bearing *torchères*, reflecting the light provided and forming an important feature of the internal architecture. Comfort became a more important consideration, and this is reflected in the increasing numbers of chairs that were completely upholstered above the legs, in Spitalfield and Genoese silks, velvet and woolen needlework, often borrowing motifs from Francis Barlow's illustrations to Ogilby's translation of the *Aeneid* and *Aesop's Fables*.

During this century, travel became more fashionable. For both patron and artist, the Grand Tour culminating in a sojourn in Rome became *de rigueur*, and this resulted in a growing awareness and appreciation of all things Italian. Indeed William Kent spent some ten years both studying and painting in Italy, where his talents came to the notice

LEFT
Pen, ink and wash design for a sidetable at Houghton by William Kent, November, 1731. For some delightfully inexplicable reason, Kent could not resist doodling clerics' heads!

of the rich, powerful and energetic Lord Burlington. In 1719 he returned to England and under Lord Burlington's influence became an architect. Both were responsible for building and decorating Chiswick Villa. Through his abilities as a designer and Lord Burlington's connections, Kent won scores of prestigious commissions ranging from the mural decorations of Kensington Palace to the decoration of Houghton, the country residence of Sir Robert Walpole. Pieces that survive include gilt chairs with Genoese silk and a fine state bed with shell head board. His furnishings for Chiswick Villa, including a fine library desk adorned with gilt owls, are now at Chatsworth. In his schemes he employed cabinetmakers like Benjamin Goodison (c.1700-67) and John Boson (fl.1720-1743).

The term 'Kentian' is used to describe a type of massive sculptural furniture, relying on pediments, masks and sphinxes. Marble slabs are often set on gilt pier-tables, in the form of a mask flanked by acanthus leaves in the case of one from Chiswick House, or Etruscan sphinxes in the cupola rooms of Kensington Palace and the saloon at Houghton. Chair backs are frequently surmounted with shells and the legs adorned with fish-scaled scrolls. The interiors illustrated in Vardy's *Designs of Inigo Jones and William Kent* (1744) are the Queen's Hermitage and Merlin's Cave, designed in about 1731 and 1735 respectively for Queen Caroline in Richmond Park. In the former a large pedimented bookcase, resembling the printed design for an organ, is placed in one arched recess and what resembles a medieval state bed, albeit with classical ornament like acanthus leaves and Vitruvian scrolls, in another. Underneath the central dome, long daybeds with curved backs are lined up in front of niches with busts of eminent thinkers on either side of the entrance. Here furniture is used to enhance the architectural symmetry. In Merlin's Cave rustic furniture is used in the form of bookcases, articulated with treetrunks rather than columns.

Kent was aware of the opportunities of mahogany, using it on a lavish scale at Houghton. Sir Thomas Robinson, in a letter to Lord Carlisle dated 9th December 1731, wrote '. . . The finishing of the inside is, I think, a pattern

for all great houses that may hereafter be built: the vast quantity of mahogany, all the doors, window-shutters, best staircase, being entirely made of that wood . . . '. Chatsworth houses two magnificent mahogany library desks from Chiswick, decorated with gilt mounts and owls, symbolic of Athene, Greek goddess of wisdom. The design for an organ, with a large central bay surmounted by a pediment and linked to the smaller bays at the side with scrolls, was repeated as a bookcase in Queen Caroline's Hermitage, and in other surviving examples. Kent died in 1748, but his influence was to survive in other pieces of furniture design, a good example being a series of massive tables from Wimpole, designed by Mathias Lock, with similar examples at Wentworth Woodhouse and Ditchley House.

Fashionable cabinetmakers of this period included Giles Grendey, Benjamin Goodison, James Moore Jr and John Channon. They were entrepreneurs who often combined a number of crafts in their businesses. Giles Grendey, for example, described himself as both chair-

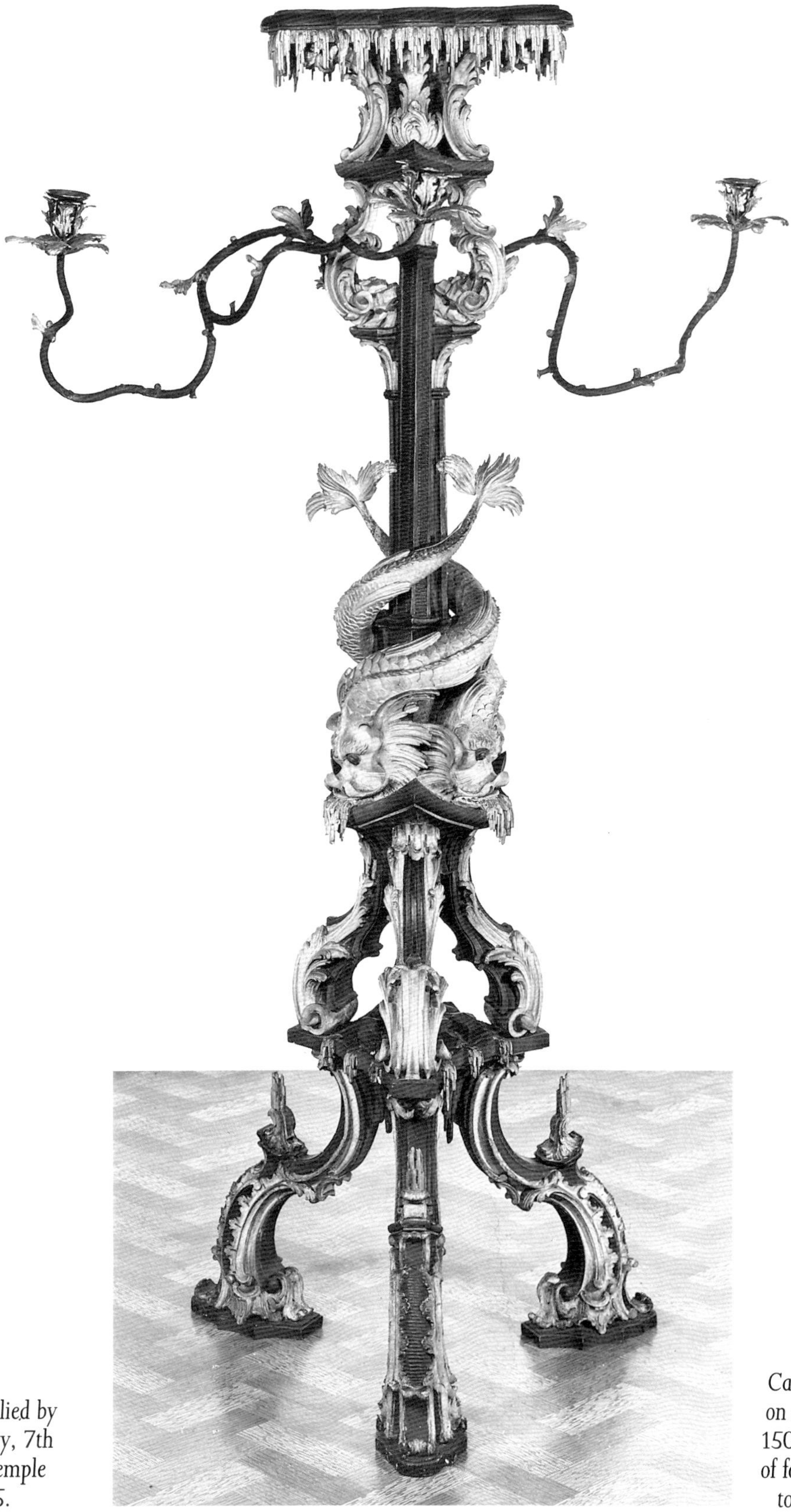

LEFT
Gilt candlestand supplied by James Pascal to Henry, 7th Viscount Irwin at Temple Newsham, 1745.

LEFT
Candlestand, about 1758, based on a design in Thomas Johnson's 150 New Designs, 1758. *A set of four candlestands were supplied to the Gallery of Hagley Hall.*

maker and cabinetmaker; as well as supplying Stourhead and Kedleston, he exported a suite of furniture to the Duke of Infantado's castle at Lazcano, northern Spain. James Moore Jr inherited his father's patrons, providing furniture for Kensington Palace to Kent's designs and enjoying the patronage of Frederick, Prince of Wales. Benjamin Goodison and John Boson were particularly connected with Kent, and the activities of William Hallet ranged from Kentian work at Badminton, Rousham and Holkham to the Gothic style for Horace Walpole at Strawberry Hill in 1755. Having made their money, craftsmen often strove for gentility. William Hallet, one of the Duke of Chandos' creditors, acquired the site of Canons, near Edgeware, in 1747, and William Bradshaw, the upholsterer, purchased land in Lancashire to which he retired.

Upholsterers mainly employed chairmakers in the first half of the eighteenth century, and in some cases still worked separately from cabinetmakers. When Lord Irwin's house in Grosvenor Square was being furnished, a separate upholsterer was brought in, although Hallet supplied the furniture. When the 4th Earl of Dysart wished to refurbish the Queen's Bedchamber, perhaps the most important room of Ham House, he turned to William Bradshaw, the tapestry maker in Soho, who specialized in tapestry and chairs with tapestry upholstery. He also used George Nix to repair old furniture and provide new pieces. By the 1740s Robert Campbell in the *London Tradesman* (1747) commented on the new type of upholsterer who 'by degrees ... set up as a connoisseur in every article that belongs to a house'. Campbell goes on to say, 'He is the man upon whose judgment I rely in the choice

ABOVE Sideboard table, c 1745, attributed to Mathias Lock, executed to a design by Henry Flitcroft for Philip, 1st Earl of Hardwicke, at Wimpole Hall, Cambridgeshire.

BELOW Elbow chair covered with Spitalfields silk, about 1730, probably supplied to Ham House by George Nix on January 1731.

of goods, and I suppose he has not only judgment in the materials, but taste in the fashions, and skill in the workmanship'.

Running concurrently with the Palladian vogue from the 1730s onward was Rococo, an expression derived from the French term *rocaille*, used to describe the recurring rock-like and shell motifs. Batty Langley, one of the first English designers to use it, described it as 'After the French Manner' in his *City and Country Builder's and Workman's Treasury* (1740). It was derived from a combination of Baroque and grotesque motifs, and developed from about 1700 onward by decorative painters such as Claude Audran and Jean-Antoine Watteau and designers of ornament such as Gilles-Marie Oppenordt, architect to the Duc d'Orléans.

One of the earliest appearances of Rococo in England was a pair of tureens made by Juste Aurèle Meissonier for the Duke of Kingston in 1735. In the same year St Martin's Academy was founded, 'principally promoted' by the painter William Hogarth, and the engravings of Hubert François Gravelot, who taught design there, did much to disseminate Rococo ornament in England. Indeed Hogarth, in his *Analysis of Beauty* (1753) called the straight line 'unnatural', advocating the S-curve as the 'Line of Beauty and Grace' – 'How inelegant would the shapes of all our moveables be without it!' Gaetano Brunetti's *Sixty Drafts of Different Sorts of Ornaments in the Italian Taste* (1736) and William de la Cour's eight *Books of Ornaments*, published between 1741 and 1748, are among the earliest Rococo pattern books in England. Brunetti's sidetables use a series of S-curves and *rocailles* but his chairs often have high backs, a feature that was by now becoming rather old-fashioned. De la Cour's chair-backs have interlacing patterns, a more elaborate version than, but still similar to, those used by clients having their portraits painted by

BELOW

Library table, one of a pair executed by John Boson for Lord Burlington at Chiswick House, 1735.

RIGHT
A dressing table, plate 118 of Thomas Chippendale's The Gentleman and Cabinet-Maker's Director (1754). *The flamboyant design is somewhat reminiscent of a dressing table by John Channon.*

ABOVE AND RIGHT
Designs for Gothic and Rococo chairs, printed in A New Book of Chinese, Gothic and Modern Chairs, (1750, 1751) *by Mathew Darly.*

RIGHT
Design for an alcove for Lady Fludyer's dressing room, Plate 85 of The Universal System of Household Furniture *by William Ince and John Mayhew,* 1759. *Lady Fludyer was the wife of Sir Samuel Fludyer, Lord Mayor of London in 1761. The 'Turkish sofa' in the alcove is an early version of the ottoman, popular in the early nineteenth century.*

Francis Hayman, who taught at St Martin's Academy.

During the 1740s Mathias Lock made fine gilt furniture, including a pier-glass and table, for the Tapestry Room at Hinton House for Earl Paulett, and also published series of designs, such as *Six Sconces*, *Six Tables* and the *Principles of Ornament*. Lock carefully studied the designs of François Cuvilliés, who trained under Jean-François Blondel in Paris and mainly worked for the Bavarian court. He borrowed Cuvilliés' designs for tables with S-curved legs, the gap between them narrowing toward the bottom, and linked with flamboyant stretchers that incorporate trophies (whether battle triumphs, as in Lock's case or gardening in Cuvilliés'!). Thomas Langley borrowed a design for a sidetable, the most striking feature being the front legs in the form of intertwined female terms , straight from a print by Nicholas Pineau, a leading French carver. James Pascal, who like Lock was a carver, produced furniture in the Rococo style, his most famous being a series of giltwood sidetables, sconces (decorative candle-holders, fixed to the wall) and seating for Viscount Irwin at Temple Newsham. The tables are very much of the Cuvilliés-Lock form. John Channon, of Exeter and London, provided furniture for Powderham Castle and Hornby Hall. The only pieces to bear his signature are a pair of monumental bookcases at Powderham Castle, lavishly decorated with ormolu mounts and inlay, and surmounted by a striking broken pediment, the design of which Chippendale could have borrowed and reused as a chamber organ. Both John Channon and his elder brother Otho subscribed to Chippendale's *Director* and, like Chippendale, John Channon had his business in St Martin's Lane and there could have been links between the two. English designers in Rococo were keen to copy French models, in an attempt to beat the French at their own game, echoing the sentiments of the hero of *The Anti-Gallican* (1757): 'Far be it from me to condemn my Countrymen for adopting any Invention in Arts or Sciences, which owes its Birth to the fertile Genius of our bitterest Enemies. No – Let us endeavor at raising ourselves to an equal, if not superior Pitch or Excellence, in every Science and Profession, to all the Nations of the Globe'.

The middle decades of the eighteenth century were marked by publication of Thomas Chippendale's *Gentleman's and Cabinet Maker's Director* of 1754, with a second edition the following year, and a response by William Ince and John Mayhew in the form of the *Universal System of Household Furniture* in 1759. Ince and Mayhew's *Universal System*, dedicated to the Duke of Marlborough, consisted of eighty-nine plates engraved by Mathias Darly with six others (of fire grates) tagged on at the end. Their designs are by and large a more cautious version of Chippendale's, particularly in regard to more extravagant pieces such a state beds and ladies' toilet tables, and there are a

good deal fewer of them. Sheraton judged the work as 'much inferior to Chippendale's'.

In 1762 Chippendale swiftly produced a third edition of the *Director*, dedicated to Prince Henry William, and also a French edition, doubtless in response to the fact that Ince and Mayhew had published their work in French. The early editions include 'household furniture in the Gothic, Chinese and Modern taste' and the third edition responds to the neoclassical ideas of James 'Athenian' Stuart, Sir William Chambers and Robert Adam, introducing motifs like ram's heads and caryatids. He included chinoiserie designs, which, as in many other French and English publications, were fantasized versions that provided a good supply of surviving ornament (fretwork for example being a widespread motif).

Mathew Darly, an engraver who styled himself 'Professor of Ornament to the Academy of Great Britain' – possibly a playful reference to the St Martin's Academy – engraved about two thirds of the first edition but the inscriptions 'T. Chippendale inv. et delin.' on the plates and one on a recently discovered visiting card of 1753 'T. Chippendale. Inv. M. Darly Sculp.' indicate that Chippendale's designs were his and not, as is sometimes suggested, ghosted.

LEFT
Pierglass and commode, part of the 'Chinese Chippendale' furniture supplied by Thomas Chippendale to Sir Roland Wynn at Nostell Priory between 1770 and 1771.

RIGHT
Dressing table by John Channon, about 1740. This fine mahogany piece is embellished with extravagant rococo gilt brass mounts. Like Chippendale, Channon's premises were in St Martin's Lane and his furniture may have influenced a few of the former's more flamboyant designs.

BELOW LEFT
Commode by Pierre Langlois, c. 1760, supplied to John Russell, 4th Duke of Bedford.

BELOW RIGHT
Gilt looking-glass supplied by Thomas Chippendale to the Duke of Portland in 1766, incorporating Rococo motifs and chinoiserie ho-ho birds.

Little is known of Thomas Chippendale's private life or formative years. He was baptized on 5 June 1718 in Otley, Yorks, the son of John Chippendale, a joiner, and married a Catherine Redshaw at St George's Chapel, Mayfair, London, on 19 May 1748. His initial training must have come from his father, and it has been argued that Richard Wood, a cabinetmaker of York who was to order eight copies of the *Director* (a larger amount than anyone other than two London booksellers), provided him with professional training. The first important payment (dated 13 October 1747) he received was from Lord Burlington 'to Chippendale in Full), £16 16 0' but what for is not recorded.

The publishing of the *Director* and the move to new and more prestigious premises in St Martin's Lane, London, combined with a financial partnership with James Rannie from Edinburgh, guaranteed success. Prestigious, even if not always lucrative, commissions resulted, such as Melbourne House in London, Wilton House, where three large pedimented bookcases, two designed by Sir William Chambers, survive, and Yorkshire commissions like Harewood House and Nostell Priory, where some of the finest examples of Chippendale's work are to be found. Letters connected with the furnishing of Nostell Priory and Mersham-le-Hatch in Kent, as well as surviving bills of the enormous range of houses (sixty-five clients have been identified to date) provide most of our information on England's most famous cabinetmaker.

Chippendale's finances were often precarious; the death of James Rannie in 1766 and the demands of his executors nearly sank the firm. The problem was aggravated by the dilatoriness of his clients in paying. A series of pleading letters to Sir Roland Winn of Nostell Priory express his fear of imprisonment for debt. In another misadventure, he was apprehended by Customs in 1769 for trying to import 60 unfinished chair frames from France. However, funds injected by Thomas Haig, Rannie's erstwhile bookkeeper and Henry Ferguson, one of his executors saved the company from bankruptcy in 1771.

The *Director* assured Chippendale's posthumous reputation and the term 'Chippendale' is often used to describe yet another clothes press with Chinese-style fretwork immediately below the cornice, work often only remotely inspired by the *Director*. Only pieces that are matched with payments and bills can be ascribed to him, although of course it is most unlikely that any pieces actually came from his own hand, after the publishing of the *Director* in 1754. The surviving pieces from his workshop range from gilt Rococo pier-glasses to inlaid commodes in the more restained neoclassical style, perhaps the finest examples being in Harewood House. Although he provided furniture to houses decorated by Adam, the only time he executed furniture to Adam's designs was at the London residence of Sir Lawrence Dundas in Arlington Street. As well as producing elaborate pieces for state

LEFT
Pedestal dressing table, about 1775, mahogany veneered with kingwood. This is an example of the use of painting and inlay on flat surfaces, as opposed to the earlier more exuberant Rococo carving, and is characteristic of Neoclassical furniture.

RIGHT
Bed hung with Indian painted cotton, about 1770, supplied to David Garrick's villa at Hampton by Chippendale. The cotton was seized from Chippendale's workshop by Customs officials and recovered with difficulty.

ABOVE
Writing table by Thomas Chippendale, about 1774, supplied to Paxton House, Berwick, Scotland, and an example of Chippendale's less extravagant furniture.

RIGHT

State bed from Calke Abbey, early eighteenth century, hung with Chinese silk and gold thread. This recently discovered bed is one of the best preserved examples of the period.

LEFT ABOVE

Detail, showing the flamboyant headboard in the style of Daniel Marot.

LEFT BELOW

Detail of the Chinese silk hangings.

apartments, he provided more simple pieces like a remarkably plain bureau dressing table and linen airer (a sort of three-leaf towel rail) for Paxton and a dining table for Nostell Priory. He also provided painted bedroom furniture in the chinoiserie (green figures on a creamy white ground) style for David Garrick. Different types of furniture called for different design. The lady of the house's toilet table would get more elaborate treatment, such as a large textile canopy, than a more practical piece like a clothes press or towel rail. Areas where visitors would congregate, such as assembly or drawing rooms, called for splendid pier-glasses to reflect the candlelight and tables to go with them, and in pieces such as these Chippendale's Rococo designs are at their most characteristically flamboyant.

The period was marked by massive architectural furniture, which had more in common with Palladio's external architecture than any pieces actually produced in Venice in the late sixteenth century. At the same time curvaceous furniture with cabriole legs and bureaus often with lacquer decoration appeared in these very houses. Gothic motifs never died out, and chinoiserie ornament developed from lacquer cabinets. Walpole and Chambers were to aim at something more authentic, in their respective styles. They will be dealt with in the next chapter. However, in circumstances where all sorts of styles were being reproduced by engravers and cabinetmakers, it can be seen that Rococo was not so outlandish and was easily adapted to English ornamentation, even if not always understood.

CHAPTER 5

Late Georgian

Neoclassical

FROM ABOUT 1760 a reaction to Rococo set in, and an alternative was sought in the close examination of classical remains, stripped of *rocaille* accretions. A more archaeological approach was adopted to the Classical. Architects and draftsmen went further afield to examine the remains of Palmyra, in the case of Robert Wood; Greece in the case of James Stuart and Nicholas Revett; and Split in Dalmatia in the case of Robert Adam. Greece, under Turkish domination, slowly became more accessible during the eighteenth century and more attractive to collectors and antiquarians, and the Society of Dilettanti financed both Wood's and Stuart and Revett's voyages. The latter resulted in the first thorough study of Greek architecture and ornament in the English language.

At the same time the search for authenticity was being applied by Horace Walpole to the Gothic. An avid collector, whose sixteenth-century 'Glastonbury chair' was one of his prize possessions, he used the surviving funerary chapels and monuments as well as illustrations from topographical works as models in the building and furnishing of Strawberry Hill, rather than content himself with craftsmen's pattern books. Indeed he dismissed

LEFT
Sidetable thought to have been designed for Buckingham House by Sir William Chambers. The top is decorated with a series of allegorical figures, possibly by G B Cipriani.

RIGHT
Armchairs in the neoclassical style and the Merman Sofas in the State Drawing Room, Kedleston, designed by John Linnell in about 1762 and executed by his workshop in about 1765. The Merfolk were used in an earlier design for a coronation coach for George III (page 86).

RIGHT
State bed at Kedleston, decorated with palm trees, designed and carved by James Gravenor in 1764.

ABOVE
Looking glass from about 1710, decorated with verre eglomisé, a technique of mounting glass with a painted and gilded background.

Batty Langley's designs as 'Bastard Gothic' and believed that 'All Gothic designs should be made to imitate something that was of that time, a part of a church, a castle, a convent, or a mansion. The Goths never built temples in a garden'. Sir William Chambers, in his capacity as a merchant, went as far afield as China and helped establish himself to no small degree through bringing back drawings of furniture and architecture from that country, which differed greatly from the fancies of chinoiserie. His *Designs of Chinese Buildings, Furniture . . .* of 1757 included bamboo chairs and tables where the dominant motif was an arrangement of compartmentalized rectangles and octagons, rather than a mixture of fretwork and grinning moustachioed and pig-tailed figures amid swirling *rocailles*.

Sir William Chambers and James 'Athenian' Stuart independently produced the first pieces of neoclassical furniture in England. Chambers had been to Rome and also Paris, where he came into contact with what was known as *le Goût Grec*. This style was originally based on Classical as opposed to Rococo ornament and called 'Greek' seemingly to appear more venerable. James Stuart produced the first Neoclassical designs for an English client, Sir Nathaniel Curzon at Kedleston, which were rejected but reused at a later date, and Chambers made the earliest surviving piece of furniture, a chair for the President of the Royal Society of Arts. This was part of a whole suite of furniture for the society's premises in Little Denmark Court that has since been lost. Chambers eschewed the cabriole leg, providing straight and tapering legs, with twisted fluting instead and also a chair rail with the Vitruvian scroll.

For George III Chambers designed a small table of satinwood, made by the Swedish cabinetmaker Georg Haupt, again with straight and tapering legs, in 1769. He designed furniture for a number of clients, including the Duke of Marlborough at Blenheim, where there survives a state bed with narrow, fluted columns and a more conservative domed tester with *rocaille* ornament, and also for Lord Melbourne at whose residence, Melbourne

RIGHT
Design for the side of a room by John Linnell, about 1755, very much in the Rococo idiom.

RIGHT ABOVE
Table, probably designed by James 'Athenian' Stuart in about 1760, for Spencer House, decorated with Neoclassical ornament such as the key batterned border on the tabletop and the fluted legs.

BELOW
Library desk at Osterley Park, about 1768, possibly made by John Linnell, with the marquetry executed by the Swedish cabinet makers Georg Haupt and Christoph Furlohg. The key patterns are characteristic of French goût grec.

RIGHT BELOW
Design by Robert Adam for the sideboard of the Eating Room at Osterley Park, 1767; note the abundance of classical ornament, a characteristic of Adam furniture.

House, his contact with Thomas Chippendale left him somewhat peeved. 'Chippendale', he wrote, 'called upon me yesterday with some designs . . . wc. on the whole seem very well but I wish to be a little consulted about these matters as I really am a very pretty connoisseur in furniture'. One of his most monumental pieces was a combined bureau, dressing table, jewel case and organ made for King Charles IV of Spain, signed by James Newham, the chief cabinetmaker of the firm Seddon and Shackleton.

James 'Athenian' Stuart published *The Antiquities of Athens* in 1762, some seven years after returning from his travels in Italy and Greece with Nicholas Revett to record the surviving monuments. He had a new repertoire of ornament at his fingertips. His earliest designs were for Kedleston, the property of Sir Nathaniel Curzon, later Viscount Scarsdale, which included Grecian tripods as pedestals for busts and pastille burners for the dining room, and a series of sidetables with straight fluted legs. These were rejected, and one suspects that Robert Adam played a part in persuading the client. Perhaps his most important commission was the interior decoration of Spencer House for Earl Spencer; the surviving furniture from the Painted Room includes the monumental lion monopode sofas, whose sides are composed of gilt lions in profile, each forming a front and back leg. They are based on Roman thrones and anticipate Percier and Fontaine's lion throne designs included in the *Recueil de Décorations Intérieurs*, the bible of the French *Style Empire*.

During the 1760s Stuart's style became more imitative of Robert Adam, although even late in life he was capable of producing something as original as the pulpit of Greenwich chapel, an elegant cylindrical structure resting on six slender Corinthian columns, a design based on the fourth century BC Choregic monument of Lysicrates in Athens, and executed by the joiners Lawrence and Arrow. With less indolence he could have beaten Le Roy in publishing the first extensive compendium on Greek architecture and decoration. Although very amiable, his lifestyle and lethargy often exasperated his patrons, not least Mrs Montagu, who took a dislike to Adam and his 'regiment of artificers' and had initially been very enthusiastic about Stuart's designs. With more energy and organization, his ideas would have had far-reaching results. Sir John Soane had in his possession a paintbox that originally belonged to the man he described as 'Poor Stuart' – in a way acknowledging a life of wasted talent.

Robert Adam returned from his grand tour in 1759, apprehensive that Stuart's Grecian designs would prove more popular with potential clients, but his professionalism and ruthless scheming, where necessary, paid off. He concentrated on ornamental detail and surviving examples of Roman interior decoration, particularly the grotesque element, providing a novelty which was to be much in demand for all Horace Walpole's strictures. In a position to expand from his father's firm in Edinburgh, his use of talented craftsmen for every element of his schemes, attention to detail and organizational abilities established him as the leading architect and decorator of his day. His ideas and the demand for them were highly influential on cabinetmakers and were responsible for some of the finest pieces to emerge from this period. Although royal patronage by and large eluded him ('my position at court or not at court . . .', as he wrote to the Earl of Buchanan in September 1781) he enjoyed a highly fashionable practice with clients including not only Lord Scarsdale but also Sir Lawrence Dundas, Lord Derby, Lord Mansfield and Robert Child. He used decorative painters such as Giovanni Zucchi and Angelica Kaufmann (who were later to marry), James Moore the carpet maker of Spitalfields, and John Linnell, not only for cabinetmaking but also upholstery. Although Adam built garden buildings and follies and added external features, such as the transparent portico at Osterley Park, where required, he was first and foremost an architect of interiors of buildings that already existed, and provided the answer for clients who wished to make radical alterations inside.

Adam's style was eclectic, drawn from what survived of ancient Roman interiors, and made use of Piranesi's ideas

ABOVE
Design for a chair of about 1765 by William Linnell. Chairs based on this design were made for Alnwick Castle and Osterley Park.

LEFT
Armchair, part of a suite designed by Robert Adam and supplied by Thomas Chippendale to Sir Lawrence Dundas's London residence at 19 Arlington Street; the only known instance of both Adam and Chippendale executing furniture designed by Adam.

ABOVE
Detail of Horace Walpole's medal cabinet; an ivory plaque of Judith with the head of Holofernes.

RIGHT
Medal cabinet of rosewood with ivory plaques, 1743, made for Horace Walpole, who by the age of 26 was an avid collector.

on the Etruscans – that they were an older civilization than the Greeks, and that Roman art stemmed from the Etruscans – without acknowledging his debt to him. Adam used motifs from excavated vases, such as those in William Hamilton's collection, to develop the Etruscan style, which included painted furniture ranging from fire screens to commodes. An Etruscan room survives at Osterley Park, but he also created them at Apsley House and Derby House, in London. Greek figures, grotesques, vases and altars were painted on a pale blue ground with black outlines. Horace Walpole dismissed it as 'painted all over like Wedgwood's ware, with black and yellow small grotesques'. Adam made disparaging remarks about the French in his *Works in Architecture* but was not averse to exploiting the possibilities of Gobelin tapestries, not only as wall hangings but also for covering settees. Tapestry rooms were included in his interiors at Croome Court, Moore Park, Newby Hall and Osterley Park. He was helped both by the cessation of hostilities at the end of the Seven Years War and the resulting craze for all things French, and also by the fact that Jacques Neilson, the superintendent of the French royal workshops, was of Scotch Jacobite extraction and spoke fluent English! Adam's attention to all matters of interior dec-

LEFT
Design for a bookcase for Lady Wynn by Robert Adam, dated July 9 1776. Note the decoration on the door panels in the Etruscan style.

RIGHT
Two Pembroke tables, plate 62 in George Hepplewhite's The Cabinet Maker and Upholsterer's Guide, *published in 1788.*

FAR RIGHT
Two Prince-of-Wales feathers chairs, plate 8 in George Hepplewhite's The Cabinet Maker and Upholsterer's Guide, *published in 1788. George Prince of Wales came of age in 1785.*

oration meant that he left a wealth of furniture designs, developing from fairly sculptural Kentian furniture to increasingly attenuated pieces with slender ornament. At the height of his popularity, he designed pieces to which he applied a wealth of Roman ornament as surface detail, whether inlaid woods, ormolu mounts or gilt gesso.

It was when Adam was losing his edge with fashionable clients that George Hepplewhite published his version of the Adam style to a more democratic clientele. Two years after Hepplewhite's death, his wife Alice published the three-volume *Cabinet Maker's and Upholsterer's Guide* (1788). The aim was 'to follow the latest or most prevailing fashion only' and adhere 'to such articles only as are of general use', and the intended public was both the cabinetmaker or upholsterer and the client (or 'mechanic and gentleman', as Alice Hepplewhite put it). The designs most closely compare with Adam's drawings of the late 1780s, sharing what was by now an attenuated quality of design. The furniture is slender and most of the decoration inlaid or painted rather than carved. Pier-glasses, for example, are simple, narrow, rectangular frames and the decoration tends to be confined to the crests. Common motifs are sunbursts, rosettes and slender festoons or drops of foliage. He made use of a variety of chairbacks, including the Prince of Wales Feathers, but died in 1786 before he could capitalize on the opportunities offered by Carlton House, the Prince's new residence. Adjustable reading desks, and a shaving table with mirror controled by a foot at the back, show that Hepplewhite was aware of the possibilities offered by gadgetry, a trend that was to grow in the early years of the nineteenth century. No mention is made of the long dining-table, which was making its first appearance at this time. Human figures, such as nymphs and putti, occasionally feature on chairbacks and the crests of pier-glasses. He reflected rather than originated the style that was to dominate amongst cabinetmakers of the 1780s and 1790s.

Adam made use of cabinetmakers such as Ince and Mayhew and John Linnell to carry out his plans. Ince and Mayhew prospered in the 1760s and 1770s and enjoyed fruitful relationships with the fashionable clients and architects of the day. With the Bedfords they worked on an exclusive basis, but in the case of the Earl of Coventry at Croome Court they worked alongside Vile and Cobb. They showed a less independent spirit toward architects than Chippendale, often following to the letter the designs of Chambers, Adam and, later, Lancelot Brown and Henry Holland. As Rococo became less fashionable, Ince and Mayhew were able to provide work in a more severe style, such as the rectilinear commodes at Coventry House or Birley, and reach high levels of skill in inlay, as is evident in the Derby House and Osterley Park commodes. For houses such as Birley they produced furniture of a more antiquarian nature. Theirs is an example of a fruitful relationship between cabinetmaker and architect, as they were able to profit from the designs of others while their own, as published in the *Universal System*, had enjoyed a less than spectacular success.

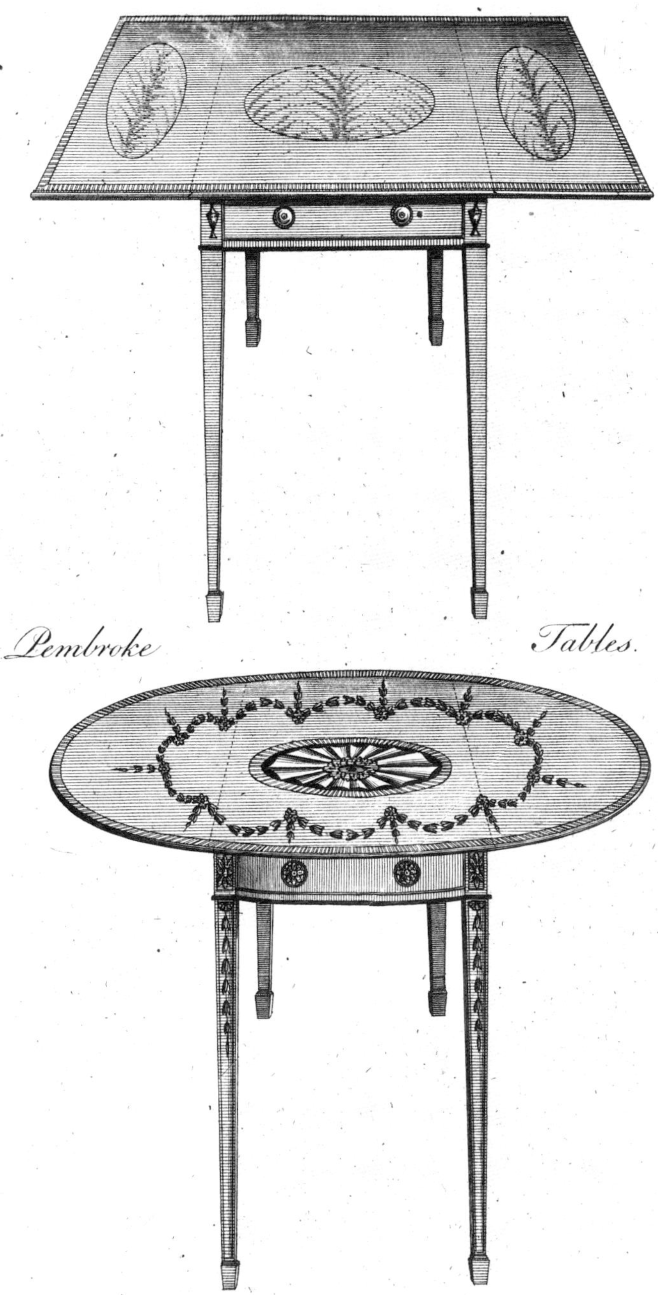

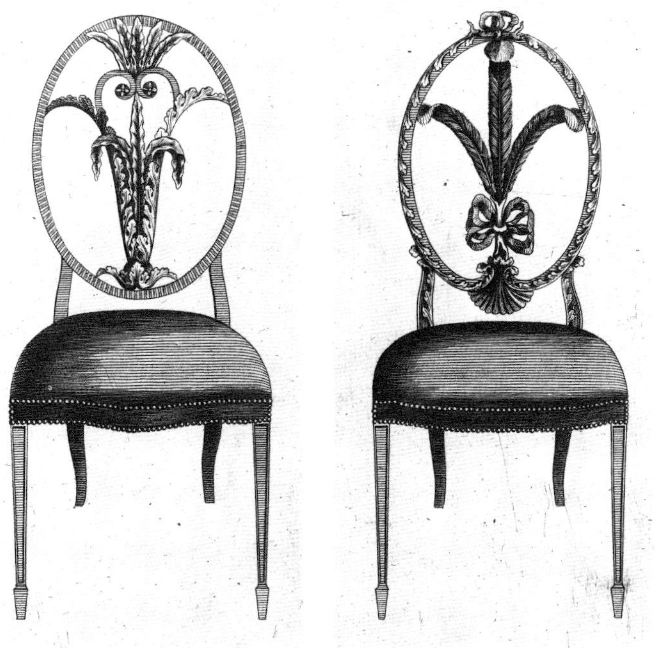

William Vile, who initially worked under William Hallet, formed a partnership with John Cobb from c. 1750 until c. 1767, when the former died. Their most prestigious work was at the royal palaces and Croome Court. They provided jewel and medal cabinets and a monumental glass-fronted bookcase for Queen Charlotte. Extensive accounts of work done at Croome Court between 1757 and 1772 include bamboo chairs, state beds, a 'handsome' commode and library bookcases. Their pieces are mixed with exuberant foliate decoration, oval wreaths on flat surfaces and fine architectural detailing, particularly on bookcases.

John Gordon and John Taitt executed important commissions during the 1770s, having formed their partnership in 1767. Gordon came from Scotland (he left a bequest to a sister in Stranraer, Galloway), where he had supplied library and bedroom furniture to the Duke of Atholl at Blair Castle and wainscoting for William, the father of Robert Adam. He kept up the Scotch connections in London, supplying furniture for the Duke of Gordon's house in Upper Grosvenor Street, although they quarreled and Gordon was left with a large unpaid bill that nearly ruined him. However, he survived this setback, and later furnished state rooms at Audley End for Sir John Griffin under Adam's supervision. Other clients included the Earl of Coventry, for whom he supplied seating and other furniture at Croome Court, and Earl Spencer, for whom it has been argued that he made the 'Athenian' Stuart lion furniture, although only a few bills, mostly for upholstery, survive. Gordon was appointed executor to Earl Spencer's will in 1778, an example of the intimacy that could exist between noble clients and their upholsterers. Gordon's death was soon to follow and in spite of their important clients, business did not prosper under John Taitt and he was declared bankrupt in 1786.

William and John Linnell (1703-63 and 1729-96), father and son, worked together from 1749 until 1763, when William died. William's early work was mainly as a carver, and his name appears on documents relating to the Radcliffe Camera, Oxford, and Woburn Abbey. His son John was a talented draftsmen, who attended St Martin's Academy and designed the chairs (and probably other pieces of furniture, as well) for the Chinese Bedroom at Badminton, for the 4th Duke of Beaufort between 1752 and 1754. These included a chair painted red, with lattice-work sides and a back surmounted with a curved pagoda roof, as well as squared but otherwise unadorned legs. The style is similar to Chippendale's 'Chinese railing', such as Chambers was to put round the outside of his Chinese temples, but had little in common with his bamboo furniture, which was decorated with compartmentalized rather than intersecting rectangles and octagons. Although no drawing has survived, John may have designed the bed, with the tester in the form of a pagoda roof with dragons at the four corners and the headboard of the same lattice as the chairbacks.

John Linnell's only published work was a *New Book of Ornament Useful for Silversmiths*. With his uncle, Samuel Butler, he designed a new state coach for George III and, although it was not executed, the fact that it was dedicated to Lord Scarsdale resulted in his producing two pairs of monumental gilt sofas for the state drawing-room at Kedleston Hall. The front legs at the side took the form of sculpted and gilt tritons and additional support was provided by two legs in between, in the form of intertwining dolphins.

John continued to use his father's premises at Berkeley Square after his death, and the sideboard and urns for the Eating Room at Osterley, although designed by Adam, were executed at this address. It has been suggested that Georg Haupt and Christopher Furlohg, two important Swedish cabinetmakers who had worked in France, produced the library furniture at Osterley, mounted with ormolu swags and inlaid with the Vitruvian scroll, characteristic of the *goût grec* which had become fashionable in that country during the 1750s. John Linnell supplied furniture to houses where Adam worked, sometimes producing his own ideas, like the triton sofas at Kedleston, sometimes those of Adam, as was the case with the sideboard at Osterley. His style, recorded in a large number of drawings, reflects a development from Chinoiserie, Rococo and Neoclassical. A colorful character, he indulged in ventures that ranged from selling prints to English settlers in India, which failed, to setting up his mistress, Polly Perfect, to defraud Lord Conyngham. His clients frequently complained of the high prices he charged for his furniture.

Foreign cabinetmakers who settled and prospered in England during this period included Pierre Langlois and Christopher Furlohg. Pierre Langlois had worked under Jean-François Oeben in Paris and settled in England in 1759. Described by Thomas Mortimer (*Universal Director*, 1763) as making 'all sorts of curious inlaid work, particularly commodes in the foreign taste, inlaid with tortoiseshell, brass, etc.', his most extensive work was at Woburn

LEFT

Table made for George III, to a design by Sir William Chambers, by Georg Haupt, 1769. An early example of Neoclassical style and the use of satinwood.

RIGHT

Kimbolton Cabinet executed by Ince and Mayhew, 1771-75, decorated with Florentine marble inlay, to a design by Robert Adam for the Duchess of Manchester. The mounts were supplied by Messrs Boulton and Fothergill of Soho, Birmingham

Abbey for the Duke of Bedford. He enjoyed a fashionable clientele that included Horace Walpole and the Earl of Coventry.

Georg Haupt and Christopher Furlohg did much to make inlaid and brass-mounted furniture fashionable. Haupt spent less than two years in England, returning to Sweden in 1769 following a royal summons, but his works include the occasional table designed by Chambers for George III and a series of library furniture done in collaboration with Furlogh in the library at Osterley Park. Christopher Furlogh, who was initially based at the Berkeley Square workshop of John Linnell, continued to produce ormolu-mounted, inlaid work with neoclassical motifs for clients who included the Duke of Northumberland, Lord Howard de Walden at Audley End and the Prince Regent at Carlton House. There are close similarities between the library table at Osterley and the billiard table at Alnwick. Both use swag-motif ormulu mounts and the inlaid Vitruvian scroll along the sides.

Toward the end of the 1760s satinwood emerged as a

LEFT

Design for George III's coronation coach by John Linnell, about 1760. Note the merfolk, which reappear on the Kedleston sofas (page 74).

RIGHT

Design for the large sofa at Kedleston Hall, about 1762.

LEFT
Library steps at Ham House, about 1750, similar to a design by Henry Keene of that date. The casters are made from a series of leather disks.

fashionable wood, the Haupt table being an early example. Satinwood came in two varieties, East and West Indian. The former did not appear on a large scale in England until the 1780s – and then was used mainly for cross-banding – but the latter was known as early as the seventeenth century. The ending of the Seven Years War in 1763 and the opening of free ports in the West Indies in 1766 made a large range of tropical woods freely available, including satinwood. Its yellow timber and lighter effect provided a pleasing contrast to mahogany, and even if this newcomer was less well suited to carving, it was excellent for inlay or painting. Specialists in inlay had before them a large repertoire of Roman archaeological ornament, made fashionable by Robert Adam who designed buildings down to the smallest interior detail. Given the detail lavished on the Harewood House commode (Chippendale), the Corsham Court commode (Cobb) or the Osterley Park Venus and Diana commodes (Ince and Mayhew), such pieces as these were clearly highly prestigious and far more than merely 'neat' and 'elegant', as they are described in Sheraton's *Cabinet Maker's and Upholsterer's Drawing Book* (1793). By the time that Sheraton was writing, East Indian satinwood was being used to cross-band and thus liven up mahogany.

Sheraton would have us believe that mahogany ruled in the dining-room and library, whereas 'neat' and 'elegant' satinwood was thought more suitable for the bedroom and boudoir. Architects such as Robert Adam were aware that the drunken noises from the eating room (as it would have been called in the eighteenth century), the male preserve, would intrude on the ladies who had left for the drawing-room. Dining chairs tended to be maho-

gany and upholstered with leather which, unlike textiles, would not retain the smell of food. This did not mean that the chairbacks could not have elaborate motifs; the Eating Room chairs at Osterley include delicately carved lyres in their design, soliciting a feeble pun from Horace Walpole about harmonizing. Chippendale thought Gothic chairs proper for the eating room, without feeling the need to explain why. Gilt chairs with damask upholstery were suitable for drawing-rooms, although gingham chair covers were more frequently on than off to protect the expensive silks.

According to Chippendale, nine chairs 'after the Chinese Manner . . . are very proper for a Lady's dressing Room', a private sitting room where she could receive people while her toilet was being completed. He also indulges in iconographical pleasantries, designing a garden chair which incorporates spades and rakes on its back, and a library chair with a dominating sunburst, indicating enlightenment, dividers and an open book. Ladies' furniture is elaborate and elegant, as one would expect, with toilet-tables adorned with silk damask hangings, as if they were state beds, and writing tables refined to the point of having few drawers for extra papers.

Practical, everyday furniture like clothes chests and presses, the eighteenth-century equivalent of the wardrobe, tended to be bulky and stripped of unnecessary ornament. Hepplewhite included a 'Plan of a Room – shewing the proper distribution of the Furniture'. In his commentary, he tells us that the drawing room should be furnished with a sofa either side of the chimneypiece, a confidante, a large sofa with separated seating at each end, and a commode between two doors, taking the place of the sideboard in the dining room. In the dining room, dining tables should be placed between windows (in fact where pier-tables would go in the drawing room and not placed in the center as a large permanent dining table, as at Carlton House), and looking-glasses, although widely used, could be omitted.

Sheraton's rule of mahogany for the dining room was by no means the universal case in the 1760s and 1770s. Christopher Furlohg made a fine satinwood inlaid side-

LEFT *Design for the state bed at Osterley Park, by Robert Adam, May 1776. 'What would Vitruvius think of a dome decorated by a milliner?' asked Horace Walpole.*

BELOW *Mahogany chair veneered with rosewood, satinwood and brass mounts made for Robert Child.*

RIGHT *Diana commode, about 1773, in the Drawing Room at Osterley Park, designed by Adam; Christopher Furlohg probably executed the marquetry panels.*

board and wine cooler for Castle Howard, dated 1767. The Eating Room at Osterley has a pair of gilt sidetables with mosaic tops, as well as a giltwood sidetable with a mahogany top. Chippendale designed 'Frames for Marble Slabs', one supported by two caryatids and with a bulbous Rococo wine cooler underneath, that would have 'a Grand Appearance, if executed with Judgment and Neatly gilt'.

From about 1770 the large dining-table, with sections and round ends, appeared. In 1771 David Garrick paid Chippendale's firm 10 10s for '2 Mahogany round ends to Join his Dining Tables, with 2 pair of strap Hinges, Hooks and Eyes, etc. 5', though the parts would probably come apart when not being used. The normal practice until the 1790s was to arrange a series of gateleg tables round the eating room and then fold them away in the passage or between the windows (i.e. against the pier) when not needed. Thomas Sheraton included an engraving of 'A Dining Parlour in imitation of the Prince of Wales' which featured a large centrally-placed dining-table, but with the chairs against the wall rather than by the table. In Jane Austen's *Emma*, only the heroine can persuade her father to abandon his Pembroke table for the new dining one. Pembroke tables, probably named after the Countess of Pembroke who is said to have made one of the first orders, were widespread from the 1760s until the 1800s. Usually of satinwood, their functions ranged from eating to work tables, and they included a number of mechanisms that enabled sections to pop up when required.

Under Adam's influence, furniture became more elongated and the architectural features were played down. From about 1770 pediments and orders tended to give way to flat tops and surface decoration with different tropical woods on bookcases. Travels abroad and the development of collecting brought about the revival of the cabinet of curiosities, in the form of the medal cabinet. As early as July 1743, Horace Walpole was writing to Sir Horace Mann 'I have a new cabinet for my enamels and miniatures just come home, which I am sure you would like. It is of rosewood, the doors inlaid with carvings in ivory'. William Vile and John Bradburn made a medal cabinet, a structure divided into three parts, for King George III in 1761, which included mahogany medal drawers and turned holes, lined with green cloth. Robert Child of Osterley Park had a marquetry inlaid medal cabinet provided, probably by John Linnell, and made by Haupt and Furlohg.

Mention should be made of Gothic. William Kent produced Gothic decorations at Rousham, the choir stall at Gloucester Cathedral and Merlin's Cave for the Princess of Wales. However, his style follows strict classical symmetry. Batty Langley included designs for Gothic chimneypieces which met with Walpole's disapproval. Gothic furniture appears in Mathias Darley's *New Book of Chinese, Gothic and Modern Chairs*, Chippendale's *Director* and Robert Manwaring's *Cabinet Maker's Real Friend and Companion*. In all cases mentioned, the designs are essentially classical and symmetrical with Gothic elements added on. Frequently Gothic and Rococo blend, as is the case with William Ince's 'Sofa in the alcove' of c. 1760 or Chippendale's Gothic library bookcase. One suspects that Pugin's designs would have been looked upon with some sympathy by Walpole but regarded as barbarous by any other connoisseur of this period. However at Strawberry Hill Walpole made a conscientious attempt to produce 'unbastardized' Gothic, based on surviving examples. The fan-vaulted ceiling of the gallery, for example, is taken from St George's Chapel, Windsor, and the library bookcases derive from side doors to the choir screen of Old St Pauls, taken from Dugdale's *St Paul's* (London, 1658), illustrated

LEFT
Sideboard and wine cooler of 1767, veneered in satinwood and other woods, by Christopher Furlohg, for Frederick Howard, 5th Earl of Carlisle, at Castle Howard.

RIGHT
Clothes press, formerly from Croome Court, designed by Adam in 1764. The doors were originally part of a four-door clothes press supplied by Vile and Cobb. Sefferin Alken executed the carving.

ABOVE
Chair from Strawberry Hill, designed by Horace Walpole and Richard Bentley and executed by William Hallet in 1755. Unlike the contemporary designs by Chippendale and others, this chair back is designed to resemble a Gothic window.

by Wenceslas Hollar. James Wyatt's building of Lee Priory for Walpole's friend Thomas Barrett was to be hailed as 'a child of Strawberry'. The building was even more asymmetrical, a quality that Walpole particularly praised. With his friend Richard Bentley, he designed a black Gothic chair for the Great Parlour, the back of which was modeled on a Gothic window, rather than some essentually Rococo mahogany chair with a few Gothic ornaments added at random. These, along with a pair of Gothic mirrors, were provided by William Hallet in September 1755. Bentley also designed a sidetable with a top of Sicilian jasper for that room, with twisted legs that harked back to Tudor furniture – one of the earliest signs of the Tudor revival. Walpole bought a set of eighteen ebony chairs from Staughton House in Huntingdonshire, convinced that they were Tudor, when in fact they were probably Indo-Portuguese.

The Neoclassical idea, first evident in Chambers' Presidential chair for the Royal Society of Arts (1759), sometimes resulted in stark, austere furniture and sometimes in highly elaborate decoration, almost as if every classical motif had to be used. In this period two trends hesitantly emerge that were to come to the fore in the next century – Grecian and Gothic. The former had its admirers and detractors but had to wait for Thomas Hope to propagate it, while an increasing awareness of Gothic art and architecture was to take on a dominant role in the next century. English furniture design was elegant and innovative on an international scale, largely through Chippendale and Adam publishing in French, the *lingua franca* of Europe.

CHAPTER 6

Regency

GEORGE PRINCE of Wales was Prince Regent from 1811 until 1820, but the furniture style associated with him began to develop in the early 1780s, flowered in the first decades of the nineteenth century and waned in the late 1820s as designers ransacked styles of the past in the vain search for novelty. The Napoleonic Wars closed off France to those who undertook the Grand Tour but turned their attention to the eastern Mediterranean, resulting in a vogue for all things Greek. On the other hand it also encouraged nationalist sentiment as regards the use of woods and English as opposed to Grecian motifs. This meant Gothic, which one writer in the *Gentleman's Magazine* thought should be renamed 'English'. Nelson's victory at Aboukir Bay and the publication of Vivant Denon's *Voyages dans la Basse et la Haute Egypte* in 1802, translated into English the same year, created a vogue for all things Egyptian for over a decade. The needs of officers and invalids helped provide a stimulus for a spate of patent furniture from about 1800 until 1820. A search for novelty and the improvements in metalworking techniques brought about by the Industrial Revolution also played their part.

Whether Gothic or classical, Regency furniture tended to be slender, elegant and economic in ornament. Brass was cheap and easily available. By about 1812 it was widely used to decorate rosewood veneered surfaces, replacing the earlier use of satinwood and ebony stringing. Cabinet furniture was often decorated with drapery held in place by the characteristic Regency wire netted patterns. 'Wire Doors' Sheraton tells us 'are much introduced at present in cabinet work . . . they have generally green, white, or pink silk fluted behind'. A relatively new piece of cabinet work was the chiffonier, so called by the French as it originally served for ladies to store their unfinished needlework, which first appeared in England in the 1770s and became a fashionable piece of furniture from about 1800. By 1808, they were low shelved cupboards and George Smith in *Household Furniture* was saying that they were 'useful chiefly for such books as are in constant use and are not of sufficient consequence for the library' and by the 1820s they were little different from commodes. Another innovation was the 'davenport', a small writing desk-cum-chest of drawers named after Captain Daven-

LEFT
Bookcase from Sheraton's The Cabinet-Maker, Upholsterer and General Artist's Encyclopedia, *published in 1806. The busts are of Charles James Fox, William Pitt, Admiral Nelson and Admiral Duncan.*

ABOVE
Armchair, about 1810, taken from George Smith's A Collection of Designs for Household Furniture and Interior Decoration, *published in 1808.*

port, for whom Gillows made a desk in the 1790s, which was to be used for much of the nineteenth century.

Brazilian rosewood, an attractive reddish-brown timber with black streaks, was first used in England in the late eighteenth century and remained popular until the 1840s. Veneering became almost universal, because it used up smaller amounts of exotic wood and enabled graining patterns to be done more economically. Carving was revived as historic styles, particularly Gothic and Tudor, came into vogue. Mahogany, although now mostly veneered except on chairs and some dining-tables, was still widely used and easily obtainable, because the dominance of the British Navy left English trading ships sufficiently protected. As early as about 1808, French polishing was being practised in England. The shellac and spirit-based substance gave it a smoother finish than earlier methods involving beeswax and turpentine or linseed oil and brick dust, and greatly enhanced the color of the wood.

Furniture was covered with a variety of woven, printed and painted fabrics, the most widely used material being chintz; it was particularly suitable for curtains, bed-hangings and seating furniture in the more informal surroundings of cottages and villas. Like calico, it was also used for cases to cover smart chairs. Patterned silk was thought suitable for Louis Quatorze furniture and serge and cloths for Gothic furniture. Horsehair and leather, particularly red or blue morocco tied down with silk straps, were considered suitable for library and dining-room chairs. Chairs were stuffed with curled horsehair, sheep's wool, chaffed hay, straw or bran, and spring seating became more common. During the late eighteenth century the ottoman made its first appearance. This could be placed against walls or be free standing and was thought particularly useful for picture galleries.

The Prince of Wales came of age in 1783, and Parliament voted him £60,000 for refurbishing Carlton House. Henry Holland, the son of a prosperous Fulham builder, was appointed architect and Francis Hervé, who had worked at Chatsworth, provided the furniture. In 1785 work stopped and a Parliamentary commission was set up to investigate the finances of this project. Two years later the Prince entered into a new and major phase of decoration, once his debts had been settled. The Prince of Wales's suppliers included Adam Weisweiler and Georges Jacob, who both worked for French royalty and were later to furnish Napoleon's palaces. Weisweiler is thought to have supplied pier-tables with curved open shelves at the side and Jacob a set of gilt chairs and settees, now at Buckingham Palace. Only two depictions survive of Carlton House; they are both of the Chinese Drawing Room in Sheraton's *The Cabinet Maker's and Upholsterer's Drawing Book*, which includes one of two pier-tables attributed to Weisweiler and a set of chairs and sofas with straight and slender legs and armrests curving down from the back rail, which may have been by Jacob. All this restrained decoration was swept away when Walsh Porter replaced Henry Holland in 1802.

The importance of Carlton House was its avant-garde nature and the fact that Sheraton, doubtless hoping to impress potential clients, chose to include it in his *Drawing Book*. It would be easier to assess if the building had not been demolished in 1827 and the furniture scattered. With the onset of war against revolutionary France, the Prince himself was concerned about his 'furniture being accused of jacobinism'. The most popular type of furniture to emerge from Carlton House was the writing desk, named after it, which appeared in Sheraton's *Drawing Book* and was repeated in the more popular *London Book of Prices* (1793), a handbook for cabinetmakers, mostly concerned with costing their work. Sir John Soane copied Weisweiler's pier-table in a design for a music cabinet for the Duke of Leeds, dated 1797, though the central section is closed with doors, and Sheraton produced a similar 'Lady's cabi-

LEFT
Design for a Carlton House lady's drawing and writing table, Plate 60 in The Upholsterer and Cabinet Maker's Drawing Book by Thomas Sheraton, 1793-94.

net', although his version stood on long straight legs linked by a shelf halfway down. The design of the Chinese drawing room *bergères* (or easy chairs), as recorded by Sheraton, was adapted to a sofa.

Holland's other French-inspired work at the end of the eighteenth century was Southill, the Bedfordshire house of Samuel Whitbread, the brewer and radical Member of Parliament. The drawing room armchairs, based on designs by Georges Jacob, are in the *Style Étrusque*, and what might be described as proto-Regency. The rear legs sweep back in a marked manner and the front ones are straight, tapered and fluted. The arms and backrests have pronounced scrolls. Other French-inspired pieces were a china cabinet in Mrs Whitbread's room, and a pair of open-shelved commodes, the latter similar to those at Carlton House illustrated by Sheraton.

Holland visited France in 1785 but never went to Italy. Instead, he sent his talented assistant Charles Heathcote Tatham, who had joined the firm in about 1789. He needed new sources of inspiration, owing to war and resulting anti-French feelings at home which made his Gallic flavor unpopular. The result of Tatham's stay in Italy (1794-97) was *Etchings and Ornamental Architecture drawn from the Originals in Rome and Other Parts of Italy during the years 1794, 1795 and 1796*. Tatham's engraving methods derived from John Flaxman's *Compositions* of the *Odyssey*, *Iliad*, and Aeschylus's tragedies, and marble monuments such as the draped seat and Roman lion marble throne provided new motifs. Roman lion monopodes appear on side tables at Southill and there exists a draped hall chair that derives from one such etching. His brother Thomas, a partner of the firm Marsh and Tatham, collaborated with Holland at Carlton House, Southill and Brighton Pavilion (1795-96).

ABOVE
Hall seat, c 1800, taken from a design by Charles Heathcote Tatham in Etchings of Ancient Ornamental Architecture drawn from the Originals in Rome and Other Parts of Italy during the years 1794, 1795 and 1796.

LEFT
Design for a sideboard, Plate 31 in The Upholsterer and Cabinet Maker's Drawing Book *by Thomas Sheraton,* 1793-94.

Thomas Sheraton, furniture designer and Baptist minister, who has become a household name owing to the furniture he did not actually make, brought out *The Cabinet Maker's and Upholsterer's Drawing Book* from 1791-94, also in three volumes. Included amid the architectural and perspectival drawing exercises were hints on the use of timbers and materials and a series of designs, ranging from kidney-shaped desks and hooded lady's writing tables, dressing tables and commodes to multi-purpose gadgetry furniture, which was to be so characteristic of this period. These include a lady's design table with a cylindrical cupboard, specially designed to accomodate a lady's hat; one with a rising screen to protect her face from the fire; and the Duke of York's library table, a very masculine piece (the strength, solidity and effect of brass mouldings) that should be mahogany rather than japanned 'as these tables frequently meet with a little harsh usage'. Pieces more suitable for ladies were often

LEFT
Sidetable designed by Thomas Hope for the Flaxman Room of his house in Duchess Street, c 1800, and featuring in his book Household Furniture and Interior Decoration, 1807.

RIGHT
Circular library table, about 1810, with legs in the form of lion monopodes, based on a design from Thomas Hope's Household Furniture and Interior Decoration, 1807.

made of satinwood with painted ovals – presumably they would get gentler treatment. The backs of Sheraton's chairs were squared and the legs reeded. Elaborate decoration was suitable for a back of a drawing-room chair, the drawing room being more the preserve of ladies, particularly after dinner. To Sheraton, 'dining-parlour' furniture should be 'substantial and useful . . . avoiding trifling ornaments and unnecessary decoration' and where men remained after dinner for serious drinking. The chairs of the dining room at Carlton House had mahogany backs and leather seating. Sheraton's *Cabinet Dictionary* (1803) included Grecian couches, animal monopodia, lion masks and chairs with the front legs curving forwards, the 'sabre' design, which was to become the standard Regency design. In his final work, *The Cabinet-Maker, Upholsterer and General Artist's Encyclopedia* (1804-6) he included Egyptian motifs, the first English pattern book to do so. This was to be lent further impetus by Thomas Hope's *Household Furniture and Interior Decoration executed from Designs by Thomas Hope* (1807).

Thomas Hope came from a rich Amsterdam banking family and went on a Grand Tour of Sicily, Greece, Turkey, Egypt, Syria, Spain and Portugal. In 1799 he purchased his house in Duchess Street, which he had completely remodeled by 1804 and preserved for posterity in the plates of his *Household Furniture*. He also owned Deepdene which he bought in 1807 and remodeled between 1819 and 1826. His aim was to propagate the Greek revival, praising 'that breadth and repose of surface, that distinctness and contrast of outline, that opposition of plain and enriched parts, that harmony and significance of

ABOVE
Chair in the form of Greek klismos and decorated in the Greek red figure vase style, c 1800.

accessories' and railing against upholsterers who 'borrowed from the worst models of the degraded French school of the middle of the last century', and furniture makers who 'were rarely initiated even in the simplest rudiments of design'. Hope's state rooms included a Picture Gallery, Flaxman Room and Lararium. He also included designs for miscellaneous pieces of furniture such as the klismos chair, the monopodium pedestal table and tripod stands as *torchères*. He drew from a variety of sources, choosing an Islamic frontispiece, Egyptian sideboards, and an organ disguised as an Ionic temple. Hope even borrowed the idea of a sleeping dog at the foot of the couch from Gothic tombs. The commentary is full of symbolism: 'Round the bottom of the room', he writes of the Flaxman Room, 'still reign the emblems of the night. In the rail of a black marble table are introduced medallions of the god of sleep and of the goddess of night'.

Hope's outline technique derives not only from Flaxman's illustrations of the *Odyssey*, *Iliad*, and Aeschylus's tragedies but also Charles Percier's *Recueil de Décorations Intérieures* which was published from about 1800 onward. Indeed he acknowledged his debt to Percier, who with Pierre François Fontaine was Napoleon's personal architect and who '. . . now devoted the latter portion of his life to the superintendence of modern subjects of elegance and decoration in France; and who . . . has not only been enabled to invent and to design the most beautiful articles of furniture . . . but has still been able, in many of the etchings which he himself has made from his compositions of this description, to improve, through the freedom and gracefulness of his touch, on the merit of the original drawings'. Not only did he approve of the style Percier introduced to the French applied arts but also the way he presented them. The most noticeable differences between the *Recueil* and *Household Furniture and Interior Decoration* was that Hope's style was less florid and his ornament less crowded, he was not concerned with imperial grandeur, and Raphaelesque grotesque did not feature in his designs. English travelers visited Paris during the Peace of Amiens (1802) and Robert Smirke, an architect, did a watercolor of Mme Récamier's bedchamber, a famous Paris interior. Those who went after Napoleon's fall were staggered by the splendor of the emperor's residences, but the English at first adopted a more chaste version of the Grecian style. It was not until after the battle of Waterloo in 1815 that the French version (i.e. that of Percier and Fontaine) became more widespread in England, an example being the supply of *bergères* (easy chairs) by Morel and Hughes to Northumberland House during the 1820s. These were lavishly ornamented and upholstered, adapted from the *Recueil de Décorations Intérieures* and harked back to the Grecian klismos.

The Hope style was largely spread by George Smith's *A Collection of Designs for Household Furniture and Interior Decoration* (1808). The work consisted of 158 colored plates and was to a large extent influenced by Hope. His style was robust and showed a fondness for ornate decoration. He is perhaps most famous for his designs of animal, particularly lion, monopodia for chair and table legs, which he did much to popularize. In 1812 Smith published *A Collection of Ornamental Designs after the Manner of the Antique*, which he based on Tatham's work. This had been republished in

RIGHT
Bergère chair, aburra wood and giltwood, derived from Percier and Fontaine's Receuil de Décorations Intérieurs *(1801-12) and supplied by Morel and Hughes to Northumberland House in 1823.*

LEFT
The Strawberry Room from Lee Priory, Kent, about 1770, which James Wyatt built for Horace Walpole's friend Thomas Barrett. Walpole, who greatly admired Wyatt's work hailed it as 'a child of Strawberry'.

1810. Other works of this period included Richard Brown's *Rudiments of Drawing Cabinet and Upholstery Furniture*, published in 1820, where symbolic prose ran riot. Cheval mirrors, we are told, can be decorated with figures of Narcissus 'to show our folly in being too much in love with our own persons'! He recommended the botanical works of Dr R J Thornton for floral ornament; dressing-tables called for the most elaborate symbolism – 'foliage and flowers producing perfumes, as bergamot, jasmines, roses, lilies of the valley, etc.' Peter and Michelangelo Nicholson published *The Practical Cabinet Maker, Upholsterer and Complete Decorator* (1826-7) which consisted of 100 colored drawings of furniture in a style reminiscent of Hope. A recurring motif was the extended scroll incorporating honeysuckle and acanthus which formed pediments to bookcases, backs of sofas and sideboards.

George Smith's *Cabinet-maker's and Upholsterer's Guide, Drawing Book and Repository* (1826) consisted mainly of Grecian furniture but also included Egyptian, Etruscan, Louis Quatorze and Gothic pieces. However, he criticized the rising tide of eclecticism, which he called 'a mélange or mixture of all the different styles associated together'. These pattern books were aimed at the cabinetmaker, upholsterer and customer, and at the same time reflect fashions in furniture. The most popular of all was the *London Book of Prices*, published at regular intervals from 1788 onward and adopted throughout the provinces. These gave the costs of different patterns and included more popular designs by Sheraton, Hepplewhite and Thomas Shearer, a rather shadowy and somewhat conservative draftsman.

Included in Hope's *Household Interior Decoration* are sideboards and couches decorated with Egyptian symbols and deities such as the winged disk of Ra, the sun god, the falcon-headed Horus and jackal-headed Anubis. Egypt seemed fabled, ancient and exotic and there were plenty of Egyptian objects to see in the Capitoline Museum after 1748. Piranesi, as well as creating an Egyptian Room in the English Coffee House in Rome, included Egyptian designs in his *Diversi Manieri d'Adornare i Cammini* (1769). Charles Tatham sent Egyptian pieces to Henry Holland, who created an Egyptian fireplace in the drawing-room at

Southill and both Sheraton and George Smith included Egyptian designs. As part of the more widespread vogue, Egyptian heads and feet came to be used as pilaster terminations on bookcases, and lotuses were widely used for sofa feet and as a double ornament dividing chair or table legs. The Egyptian vogue was at its height in about 1810 but terms like 'barbarous' came to be applied to it as it fell from fashion.

The refurbishment of Carlton House heralded a Chinoiserie revival – as far as we can tell from the Sheraton engravings, more in the spirit of Rococo fantasies than Chambers' accurate observations. However, Henry Holland designed a Chinese dairy for the Duke of Bedford at Woburn Abbey in about 1790, following the more geometric nature of the furniture in Chambers' *Chinese Designs*. Furthermore the Brighton Pavilion, at which work began in 1802, had imported Chinese furniture in the Long Gallery. Elward, Marsh and Tatham were to provide English pieces in Chinese style, such as simulated bamboo dining chairs and a small commode of painted beach with bamboo skirting. The dining chairs had a Gothic chair rail, cane seating and, despite the simulated bamboo effect the legs – straight at the front and curved backwards at the back – follow the normal English pattern. Bamboo pieces made popular bedroom furniture and commodes with black and gold lacquered panels were also fashionable. However, closer association with China dispelled legends of Cathay and disillusion followed. The chinoiserie decoration at Brighton Pavilion was among the last of the kind. The opening up of Japan, half a century later, was to provide the new oriental mania.

Gothic architecture and ornament was treated with enthusiasm by the *Gentleman's Magazine* and gave rise to grand building schemes such as Lee Priory, Luscombe Park, Fonthill Splendens and Windsor Castle. George Smith may have had these in mind when he referred to the 'many mansions of the Nobility and Gentry' with regard to his design for a gothic state bed. In addition, an increasing enthusiasm for the country and nature (as well as the gains to be had from 'improving the estates') went hand in hand with picturesque small gothic country houses known as villas or cottages or the *cottage orné* in a remoter part of a large estate. The tendency to accommodate servants in an adjoining wing rather than in the basement meant that rigid symmetry was less practical and, as Horace Walpole found out, Gothic buildings did not have to be symmetrical. This vogue was extended to suburban villas, popular with merchants and professionals who wanted somewhere more rural to return home to after business. Ackermann's *Repository* (September 1813) illustrated a Gothic chair 'not in unison with the refined and classic taste of modern times: the very circumstances probably make this design analogous to the purpose of a cottage orné'. The pattern books mentioned above included Gothic designs, particularly from the mid 1820s onward. J B Papworth's *Designs for Rural Residences* (1818) and P F Robinson's *Designs for Ornamental Villas* (1827) gave Gothic a stimulus, with Robinson offering eleven styles for villas, seven of which were medieval or Tudor.

In 1826 Nicholas Morel was appointed to furnish the royal apartments at Windsor in the Gothic style. Augustus Welby Pugin's unpublished diary of 26 June 1827 reads

LEFT
Rosewood cabinet with brass decoration and a Mona marble top about 1815, attributed to George Bullock. Bullock owned the Mona marble quarry in Anglesey, and used it to embellish his furniture.

LEFT
The state bed at Badminton House, designed by John Linnell, about 1752-54, in the Chinoiserie style for the 4th Duke of Beaufort.

ABOVE
Couch, one of a pair, about 1800, designed by Thomas Hope for the Egyptian Room of his London residence in Duchess Street, and illustrated in Household Furniture and Interior Decoration, 1807.

LEFT
Sidetable, decorated with 'buhlwork', about 1820. This is an example of the vogue for boulle decoration of the time of Louis XIV, which was popular with both Napoleon and the Prince Regent.

'went to design and make working drawings for the Gothic furniture at Windsor Castle at 1 1s per day for the following rooms. The long gallery, the coffee rooms, the vestibule ante-room, halls, grand staircase, octagon room in the Brunswick tower and the Great Dining-Room'. The surviving furniture, mainly from the dining room, includes rosewood sideboards and dining chairs picked out with gilding. Twenty-four of these were sent to furnish the Throne Room of Buckingham Palace in 1834.

Perhaps the most famous cabinetmaker of the period, and one very much enjoying a vogue at the moment, is George Bullock. He was most famous for the use of native materials for fashionable furniture and native plants as decoration. The furniture for the Duke of Athol was made from the larch on the estate of Blair Castle. Bullock also owned a marble quarry in Anglesey that provided green Mona marble tops. He presented himself as a good patriot as well as a man of taste, who revived nationalist styles such as Elizabethan. His clients included Sir Walter Scott, and perhaps his most prestigious undertaking was to produce English wood furniture for the deposed Emperor Napoleon's residence at Longwood, St Helena. Bullock was an enthusiastic user of boulle (or buhl as the anglicized version was), perhaps too enthusiastic for

Richard Brown who felt that 'many of his articles were overcharged with buhl'. Boulle decoration, named after the great French ebeniste André-Charles Boulle (1642-1732) and consisting of cut brass inlaid with tortoiseshell or shellac, was encouraged by the Prince Regent's love for it and enjoyed a vogue in England in the early nineteenth century. George Oakley and Louis Le Gaigneur provided the Prince with furniture of this style. Bullock produced dwarf boulle cabinets with Louis Quatorze forms, a style that will be discussed in the next chapter. George Siddon struck a patriotic note in the *Cabinet Maker's Guide* of 1830 by saying that although it 'had hitherto been monopolized by foreigners' he was sure that 'British artists will equal if not outdo their rivals'. As the Louis Quatorze style became more fashionable in the late 1820s the patterns became more florid, after a restrained, classical beginning.

Another famous cabinetmaker of the period was George Seddon & Sons, perhaps the largest firm in London at the end of the eighteenth century. In partnership with Nicholas Morel, they provided Gothic furniture

LEFT
Sidetable, c 1805, designed for the Gothic library at Stowe, probably by Sir John Soane. Gothic furniture with monastic connotations was increasingly thought to be suitable for libraries in the early nineteenth century.

RIGHT
Joseph Bonomi's design for a dining table at Lambton Hall, Co. Durham, about 1782. The large centrally placed dining table was still something of a novelty.

BELOW
Cabinet veneered with maple and ebony, about 1815, probably by George Bullock. By 1815 the use of local woods was thought patriotic, and Bullock was able to capitalize on this.

ABOVE
Armchair, c 1835, designed by Benjamin Dean Wyatt for Lancaster House, which he decorated in the Louis Quatorze style for the Second Duke of Sutherland. This chair, however, is more in the style of Louis Quinze!

for Windsor Castle for £180,000 between 1827 and 1833, to Pugin's designs, gaining a certain notoriety when Parliament initially refused to pay more than the balance owing to their first estimate. However, the royal connections and Ackermann's enthusiasm for Pugin's designs did much to make Gothic fashionable. Marsh and Tatham, later to become Bailey and Saunders, provided furniture for Carlton House and Brighton Pavilion. Other fashionable clients included the Duke of Bedford and Samuel Whitbread.

Between 1790 and 1830, large amounts of 'patent' furniture were sold. Expanding dining tables such as Richard Gillow's telescopic dining table or William Pocock's 'Patent Sympathetic table' were most popular. So were reclining and invalid chairs, such as Joseph Merlin's mechanical chair, and library gadgets such as revolving bookcases, tables that turned into steps and Campbell's library steps, which were hidden in a chair and first made for George III, a great bibliophile. A multi-purpose, expanding table was useful for owners of more modest means, who used the same piece for breakfast and formal dinners, and a revolving bookcase provided a useful storage solution for those who could afford books but not a library of bookcases. However, they were also popular with the rich, and a delight in gadgetry rather than the need to save on space seems to have been the main motivation.

A number of patents were issued for improvements that involved brass, such as William Bay's extending tubes and Samuel Pratt's metal spring frame rods for bed hangings (1825), while Thomas Breidenback patented a close-mesh metal wire for testers, sackings, bed enclosures and coverings to obviate the 'annoyance of mosquitoes and other vermin'. By 1833, Loudon found iron bedsteads were 'to be found in the houses of people of wealth and fashion in London, sometimes even for best beds'. However, brass, vermin-free bedsteads aside, demand for 'patent' furniture had declined by the 1830s.

Amid the disparate elements, the dominant theme in the period was the personality of George IV, a monarch passionately interested in the arts, particularly when it came to decorating his residences, even if his extravagance resulted in a succession of financial crises and left his architects and upholsterers frustrated by schemes abandoned and bills not paid. As early as 1784 Colonel Hotham, the Prince's treasurer and secretary, wrote 'It is with equal grief and vexation that I now see your Royal Highness . . . totally in the hands, and at the mercy of your builder, your upholsterer, your jeweller and your tailor'. Three years before his death, Mrs Arbuthnot, wife of the Tory MP Charles Arbuthnot and friend of the Duke of Wellington, was writing in her journal 'The King has the greatest contempt for the Ministers but thinks of nothing but upholstery and his fine buildings . . . .' The English tend to name their furniture periods after their kings and queens, but if any sovereign deserves to be remembered by the style associated with him it is the Prince Regent, later George IV.

CHAPTER 7

Early Victorian

AFTER THE death of George IV a wide variety of styles remained available. Somewhat massive furniture in the contemporary or Grecian style continued to be produced, and at the same time a number of historical revivals, both nationalist and French, took place. The opulent Louis Quatorze style was used by Benjamin Dean Wyatt at Apsley House and Crockford's Gaming Club, and by Philip Hardwick at the Goldsmiths' Hall. Pugin was busy reinterpreting Gothic furniture, basing his ideas on surviving fifteenth-century examples. In about 1835 Thomas Hopper created Norman-style interiors and furnishings for Penrhyn Castle, the North Welsh property of the slate magnate G.H. Dawkins Pennant. Henry Shaw's *Specimens of Ancient Furniture* (London, 1836) and T.F. Hunt's *Exemplars of Tudor Architecture Adapted to Modern Habitations* (London, 1830) helped foster an interest in antiquarianism and furniture in period styles, as did the brief descriptions of historic houses that regularly featured in Ackermann's *Repository* and Joseph Nash's *Mansions of England* (1839-1849), complete with illustrations of interiors of 'olden times'. Exhibitions such as the Great Exhibition (1851) and the International Exhibition of London (1862) provided further opportunities for cabinetmakers to display their virtuosity and architects their novelties.

By this time comfort had become a prime requirement. When Barbara Hofland visited Ham House in the 1830s, her comment (published in *Richmond and its Surrounding Scenery*, 1831) on the Duke of Lauderdale's tastes, some 150 years earlier, was, 'There is an appearance of grandeur beseeming the polished nobleman . . . though he has not reached the acme of present elegance. The luxury of ease is rarely compatible with the display of labored pomp and exuberant ornament'.

The 'luxury of ease' was enhanced by Samuel Pratt, who in 1826 and 1828 brought out patents for spiral springs that he used for seats and chairs. In the eighteenth century this process had been confined to gymnastic chairs such as William Vile's 'Chamber Horse'. Pratt supplied furniture to Stafford House and Stoneleigh Abbey as well as to the Royal Household. From about 1830 squab seating was replaced by spiral springs, which were being

LEFT
Wardrobe, about 1835, designed by Thomas Hopper in the Norman style as part of his schemes for Penrhyn Castle, the North Welsh property of the slate magnate G H Dawkins Pennant.

RIGHT
The Yateman cabinet, 1858, designed by William Burges and painted by E J Poynter for H G Yateman. This is derived from a thirteenth-century painted medieval armoire at Noyon, and is one of the earliest of a series of painted cabinets in this style executed during the late 1850s and early 1860s.

XXX

LEFT
Firescreen from Keith Hall, Scotland, in the Tudor Revival style, 1850, by Jennens of Bettridge, who manufactured papier mâché in Birmingham.

RIGHT
Fly-chair painted white and gilded, in the Louis Quatorze style of about 1834, designed by Philip Hardwick for the Court Drawing Room of Goldsmiths' Hall.

FAR RIGHT
Armchair in the Tudor Revival style of about 1835, although borrowing a great deal from the high-back chairs of the 1670s.

made by the hundredweight in Birmingham by 1833. In about 1850 deep buttoning was introduced to England by Viennese workers and a variety of seats developed; these included the *pouffe*, a cylindrical stool with no woodwork showing, and the *confidant*, a series of seats, usually two or three forming an S-curve or four forming a merry-go-round. Such comfort gave rise to 'lounging', a habit condemned by Captain Orlando Sabertash. 'All these vile and distorted postures,' he wrote, 'must be reserved for the library couch or arm chair, and should never be displayed in the society of gentlemen, and still less in that of ladies!'

In his *Encyclopedia of Cottage, Farm and Villa Architecture and Furniture* (London, 1832), John Loudon wrote, 'The first or modern style is by far the most general, and the second Gothic or perpendicular has been more or less the fashion in Greek houses from the commencement of the last century; since which period the third and fourth [i.e. Elizabethan and Louis Quatorze] are occasionally mixed, and the demand for them is rather on the increase than otherwise'. 'Grecian' style was based on Regency patterns and was fashionable for dining rooms and clubs well into the 1840s, with Henry Whitaker designing Grecian furniture for the Conservative Club in 1844 and Philip Hard-

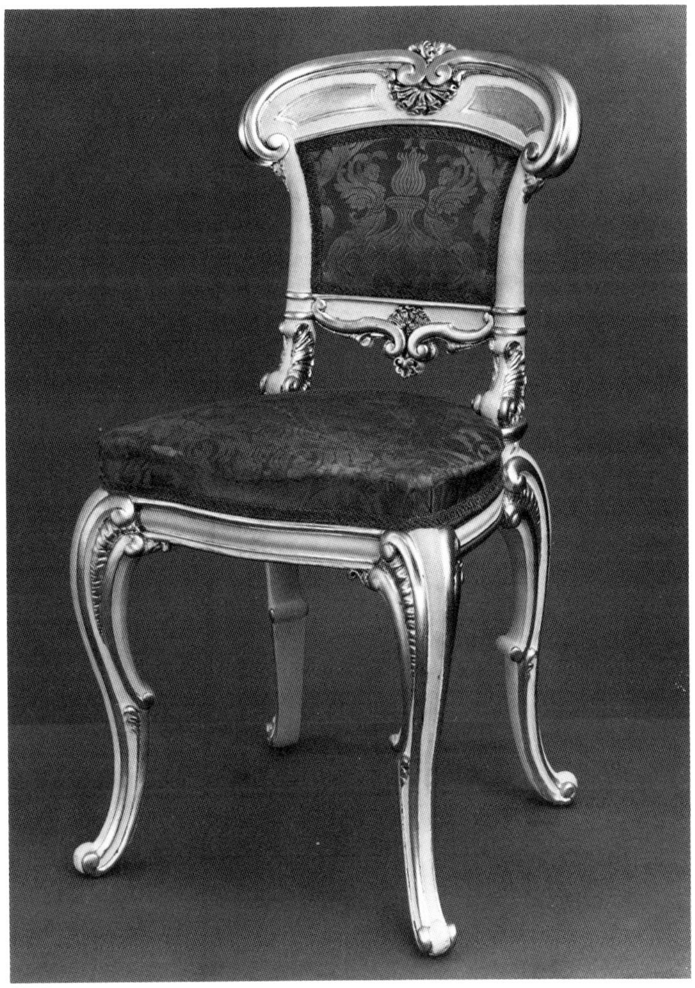

and 'Old French' interiors at Apsley House, Belvoir Castle, Tatton Park, York House (later Stafford House) and Crockford's Club. Thomas King used the style to evoke 'the French taste for lightness and elegance' and Benjamin Dean Wyatt was prepared to defend it in court. What was called Louis Quatorze in fact embraced the styles of Lous XIV, XV and XVI; and one chair from Stafford House is closest to Louis Quinze in style. On a mass-produced level, this ornament was widely applied to papier mâché objects such as chairs, loo tables (named after a card game) and trays. Papier mâché was made from layers of rag paper glued together, japaned and decorated with mother-of-pearl and oil gilding. Such objects were displayed at the large international exhibitions and the initial enthusiasm was such that they might have supplanted wood, but they proved too brittle and such pieces as have survived tend to have wooden cores.

At the same time Henry Shaw helped develop the 'Olde English' style with his *Specimens of Ancient Furniture drawn from Existing Authorities by Henry Shaw FSA, with Descrip-*

wick doing likewise for the Goldsmiths' Hall. Massive sideboards, surmounted with scrolled acanthus pediments, continued in more ornate forms well into the 1840s and the crests of chairs extending beyond the uprights in Regency fashion were rounded at the ends. Loudon's comments belie any impression that Gothic was supplanting the classical. The main propagator of this style was John Buonarotti Papworth (the middle name adopted in 1815) who had been active from the 1790s onward. His work ranged from Ackermann's new premises in 1826 to a glass throne for the Shah of Persia, and he worked for a number of cabinetmakers in the 1830s, such as Edward & William Snell, George & Thomas Seddon and Thomas Dowbiggin. He regularly contributed to Ackermann's *Repository* from 1812 to 1823, and his publications included *Rural Residences* (1818, second edition 1832) and *Hints on Ornamental Gardening* (1823). He also brought out the fourth edition of Sir William Chambers' *Treatise on Civil Architecture* in 1826. He was influential in the setting up of the new government School of Design, which opened in 1837, although he resigned a year later. While he praised Percier and Fontaine, he condemned the Rococo revival, as practised by Hardwick and Wyatt.

As well as his Grecian furniture, Philip Hardwick designed the white and gold drawing-room furniture in 1834 for the Goldsmiths' Hall in the Louis Quatorze style. Surviving chairs incorporate motifs like the cabriole leg and *rocaille*, and in one example the chair rail extends beyond the upright in the Regency fashion, despite the abundance of Rococo motifs. Benjamin Dean Wyatt, son of the fashionable James Wyatt, designed Louis Quatorze

Hall, Birmingham (1819-24), for James Watt. The design for the sideboard he included in his *Furniture with Candelabra and Interior Decoration* (London, 1838) along with twenty-six other Elizabethan designs, which helped popularize the style. The Aston Hall examples borrow the Elizabethan drawer-table, but also feature scrolls and fluted ornament. The wine cooler (or cellaret) incorporates Elizabethan strapwork and masks but has a pine-cone finial at the top of the lid, as might be expected of an object in the Grecian style. The sideboard is a heroic attempt at Northern European sixteenth-century motifs, incorporating strapwork and herms and yet, despite the surface ornament, the structure, typical of the early nineteenth century, could just as easily have been executed in the Gothic or Grecian styles. Not that this would have worried the potential client unless he happened to be a dedicated antiquarian. 'Tudor' furniture often relied on an abundance of strapwork, Tudor Rose rosettes and cut-gem motifs, and its popularity owed much to nationalistic sentiments. Furthermore, there was always the chance of winning over clients with a style which could provide comfort in harmony with a sixteenth-century residence. Sir Walter Scott's romantic novels such as *Kenilworth* (1821) also encouraged the trend and his name was applied to the 'Scott' chair, a high-backed seventeenth-century inspired model, at the time regarded as Elizabethan.

Augustus Welby Northmore Pugin, whose work at Windsor Castle has already been mentioned, published a collection of designs entitled *Gothic Furniture* in 1835, which included among the more fanciful designs a

tions by Sir Samuel Meyrick, published in 1836. Some of his examples have since been treated as suspect, particularly as quite a number belonged to the dealers John Webb and John Swaby. T. F. Hunt's *Exemplars of Tudor Architecture* was favorably reviewed by the *Quarterly Review* (July 1831), which found Elizabethan furniture 'highly rich and elegant . . . and capable of easy adaptation to all the luxurious wants of our most fastidious Sybarites''. Indeed Anthony Salvin, who designed Elizabethan sets of furniture at Malmhead in Devonshire (1827-33) and Scotney Castle in Kent (1835-43), unsuccessfully submitted designs for the Houses of Parliament in this style. From Thomas Bott, the fashionable cabinetmaker and upholsterer of St Margaret Street, Cavendish Square, the Lucy family acquired Elizabethan furniture for the dining room at Charlecotte Park, Warwickshire and Gillows furnished an Elizabethan bedroom for the Tempest family, at Broughton Hall, Yorks.

Richard Bridgens worked on the interiors of Aston

LEFT
Cabinet in the Renaissance style incorporating Mulready's Crossing the Brook, *about 1850. Designed by Gottfried Semper and executed by Holland & Sons, it was exhibited at the Paris exhibition of 1855.*

LEFT
Chair designed by A W N Pugin and supplied by J.C.Crace to Scarisbrick Hall for Richard Scarisbrick, about 1840.

RIGHT
Painted writing bureau, about 1858, with open bookshelves and gables, designed by Norman Shaw and made by James Forsyth, and exhibited in the London International Exhibition of 1862.

simple X-frame chair and stool, each held together with a through tenon secured by an unconcealed peg, pointing the way to 'honest construction'. His views on furniture were outlined in *The True Principles of Pointed or Christian Architecture* (London, 1841). Condemning unnecessary ornament such as 'staircase turrets for inkstands, monumental crosses for light-shades...', he poured scorn on upholsterers who chose '...flying buttresses about an armchair ... innumerable mitres, sharp ornaments and turreted extremities'. He added, 'a man who remains for any length of time in a modern Gothic room, and escapes without being wounded by some of its minutiae, may consider himself very fortunate'. He did not admire Walpole's applying of Gothic funerary monuments to a domestic setting at Strawberry Hill but admitted that he himself had 'perpetuated many of these enormities in the furniture I designed some years ago for Windsor Castle. At that same time I had not the least idea of the principles I am now explaining.' These he outlined in the opening paragraph of his lecture as '1st, that there should be no features about a building which are not necessary for convenience, construction and propriety, 2nd that all ornament should consist of enrichment of the essential construction'. His first important architectural commission was Scarisbrick Hall, for Richard Scarisbrick. His most extensive decorative scheme was the New Palace of Westminster, the furniture being made by Holland & Sons, Gillows, and J.C. Crace, the last of whom was to advertise in *The Builder* (1851) 'Ancient House Furniture ... executed under the immediate supervision of Mr A.W. Pugin, Architect'.

A cabinet bookcase designed by Pugin, made by J.C. Crace and acquired by the South Kensington Museum (now the Victoria and Albert Museum) a year later was hailed as one of the most important pieces in the Medieval Court at the Great Exhibition of 1851, and the original intention may well have been to fit it up in Crace's show room. In the reports by the jury, Richard Redgrave, Art Superintendent at the South Kensington Museum, praised the '... carved oak bookcase by J.C. Crace and other works. These are particularly to be commended for their sound constructive treatment, and the very judicious manner in which ornament is made subservient to it'. This carved oak piece was modeled on the medieval armoire, decorated with fifteenth-century Gothic tracery and interlacing patterns (often found on panels of the time) on the side doors, and brass ornament, incorporating scrolls, foliage and tracery, forming a grill to the central doors. Redgrave ended on the optimistic note 'some credit... is due to the revival of a better and purer state of things, and a return to the old paths and avoidance of the present mere sensualism of ornament'.

The Great Exhibition of 1851 was the culmination of a series of exhibitions held in the late 1840s by the Royal Society of Arts. It was largely brought about by the encouragement of the Prince Consort and the organizing abilities of Sir Henry Cole, a civil servant and entrepreneur at the forefront of attempts to improve design. Furniture was exhibited in Class 26, being officially described as 'Furniture, Upholstery, Paper Hangings, Papier Mâché and Japaned Goods'. The firms that took part included J.C. Crace, Holland & Son, Gillow & Co, Graham & Jackson and provincial firms such as H. Eyles of Bath and Jennens & Bettridge of Birmingham.

Despite the general euphoria and huge profits – large enough to finance the founding of the South Kensington Museum, forerunner of both the Victoria and Albert and Science Museums – there was a feeling among critics that good design was still lacking. *The Times* commented in a leading article that '... it seems to us that the art manufacturers of the whole of Europe are thoroughly demoralized'.

International exhibitions such as the Great Exhibition and those that followed gave rise to showpiece cabinets, built on a massive scale so as not to be dwarfed by their surroundings, and certainly not for domestic settings. At the Paris exhibition of 1855 Messrs Jackson & Graham exhibited a huge cabinet designed by their French employee, Eugène Prignot. This manifesto of English applied arts consisted of Minton plaques, Birmingham ormolu mounts and London cabinetmaking. 'Such a result' stated the catalogue '... reflects the highest credit upon all engaged in the production of this elegant specimen of art-manufacture, and it demonstrates the fact that works of an ornamental character, and of the highest degree of excellence, can be made in this metropolis'. Other English cabinetmakers represented at the Paris Ex-

LEFT

Cabinet bookcase designed by Pugin, made by J.C.Crace and exhibited in the Medieval Court at the Great Exhibition of 1851. The design derives from armoires of the fifteenth century.

BELOW

The René of Anjou cabinet, about 1861, designed by J P Seddon and consisting of panels painted by William Morris, Edward Burne-Jones, Dante Gabriel Rossetti and Ford Maddox Brown; exhibited in the London International Exhibition of 1862.

hibition included Holland & Sons, who displayed a cabinet (on a considerably smaller scale than Jackson & Graham's) in the Renaissance style which incorporated Mulready's painting *Crossing the Brook*. It was designed by the German architect Gottfried Semper, who was responsible among other things for The Duke of Wellington's funerary car.

The 1862 London International Exhibition brought the Gothic painted furniture of William Burges, William Morris, Edward Burne-Jones and Ford Madox Brown to prominence. Figurative painted furniture, often illustrating a medieval poem or legend or even something playful like the battle between wine and ale, provided a radical departure from varnished wooden surfaces, whose main ornament was either inlay or the natural graining pattern, and catered for a widespread enthusiasm for all things medieval. At the International Exhibition of 1862, Morris & Co. managed to sell £150 worth of goods which included stained glass, embroideries, tiles, table glass, candlesticks and indeed furniture, and to win two gold

LEFT
Cabinet with pierglass designed by Eugène Prignot and executed by Jackson and Graham, exhibited at the Paris Exhibition of 1855. This served to advertise the best in English applied arts; Minton plaques, Birmingham ormolu mounts and London cabinetmaking.

BELOW
Detail of Edward Burne-Jones's cabinet, opposite.

medals. 'Messrs Morris & Company,' stated the jury reports, 'have exhibited several pieces of furniture, tapestries etc, in the style of the Middle Ages. The general forms of the furniture, the arrangement of the tapestry, and the character of the details are satisfying to the archaeologist from the exactness of the imitation, at the same time that the general effect is excellent.'

Examples of work exhibited by Morris & Company included the St George Cabinet designed by Philip Webb in 1861 and painted by William Morris, and the René of Anjou cabinet designed by J.P. Seddon and consisting of panels painted by Morris, Burne-Jones, Rossetti and Ford Madox Brown. The St George Cabinet was a long rectangular structure set on a stand with turned legs. It was divided into three parts and closed at the front by doors on which Morris himself painted scenes from the life of St George. The René of Anjou Cabinet was described in the illustrated catalogue of the London International Exhibition of 1862 as 'a case of shelves for drawings and prints – to serve also as a portfolio rest'. This would explain the large reading stand set above the doors. The doors illustrate the honeymoon of King René, with different lovers' poses symbolising Architecture, Painting, Sculpture and Music.

Other painted cabinets that featured in the International Exhibition included a painted writing bureau with open bookshelves surmounted by Gothic gables, designed by Norman Shaw and made by James Forsyth, and a humorous cabinet entitled the Battle of the Wines and Beers (Sir Bacchus v Sir John Barleycorn), designed by William Burges (1827-81) and painted by Sir Edward Poynter. One of the earliest of these painted cabinets was the Yateman Cabinet of 1858 designed by William Burges, who had been inspired by two surviving thirteenth-century pieces of painted medieval French furniture at Noyon and Bayeux, illustrated by the great French medievalist, Viollet-le-Duc. He admitted, 'we all cribbed from Viollet-le-Duc'. He trained as an architect and helped prepare *Domestic Architecture of France* with Henry Clutton; his polychrome designs for the organ case at Lille Cathedral anticipated the style of his furniture.

William Morris was the son of a rich stockbroker from Walthamstow, and formed a friendship with Edward Burne-Jones at Oxford University. Despite his own failure to become an architect, he made friends with the successful architect Philip Webb, who was to become what Ros-

ABOVE LEFT

Cradle designed by Norman Shaw, 1867, for Julian, the second son of Alfred Waterhouse, and decorated with the signs of the zodiac.

LEFT

Cabinet on a stand, about 1860, with an allegorical subject painted by Edward Burne-Jones and originally owned by the artist.

setti described as one of 'our most active men of business as regards the actual conduct of the firm' of Morris & Co. Morris formed a business partnership in 1861, at the suggestion of Ford Madox Brown, to produce well-designed and executed decorative work, the catalyst being the decoration of the Red House designed for Morris by Webb, where he moved after his wedding. In 1865 Morris moved to Queen's Square, Bloomsbury, and carried on the business there. His most important commissions following the International Exhibition of 1862 were the decoration of the Armory and Tapestry Room at St James's Palace (1866-67) and the Green Dining Room of the South Kensington Museum (1867). Unlike Ford Madox Brown, Morris himself designed little furniture, other than solid practical pieces in his workshops in Red Lion Square in his early days in London. Larger pieces such as settles tended to be conceived as a series of flat surfaces suitable to be painted on by friends such as Burne-Jones and Poynter. A few later examples included a semicircular chair at which he sat while weaving, and the Sussex chair, which was adapted from an already existing piece of simple rural furniture; this was an armchair with simple, turned legs of stained wood, rushed seating, and the chairback rails linked with spindle-like ornaments.

On the whole Morris was more interested in textiles and wallpapers such as Daisy, Trellis and Fruit (1864) and Tulip and Willow (1873), his first chintz, than in furniture. This did not, however, stop him from expressing his views on furniture, which he felt should fall into two categories, 'necessary workaday furniture' and 'state furniture'. The first should be 'simple to the last degree' and as for the second, 'we need not spare ornament on these, but make them as elegant and elaborate as we can with carving or inlaying or painting; these are the blossoms of the art of furniture'. Warington-Taylor, his business manager, made pleas for 'moveable furniture, light . . . something you can pull about with one hand'.

BELOW
St George Cabinet, designed by Philip Webb in 1861 with scenes from the life of St George and painted by William Morris. This long rectangular structure was divided into three parts, closed at the front by doors. It was exhibited at the International Exhibition of London, 1862.

LEFT
Detail of the St George Cabinet.

RIGHT
Drinks cabinet showing the Battle of the Wines and Beers (Sir Bacchus v Sir John Barleycorn), designed by William Burges and painted by Sir Edward Poynter. It was exhibited at the International Exhibition of London, 1862.

A.W. Pugin, William Burges, Charles Bevan and Norman Shaw did much to popularize their different interpretations of the Gothic style. Pugin preferred the more attenuated and perpendicular qualities of English fifteenth-century style, so long as ornament formed 'the decoration of Construction', while the other three adopted a style based on that of the French thirteenth century, with its more bulky and less pointed qualities and painted surfaces. Following Pugin's furnishing of the House of Lords there was something of a Gothic vogue, with J.C. Crace advertising furniture of this style made under the architect's supervision in *The Builder*, and yet a workaday pattern book like P. Thomson's *Cabinet Maker's Assistant* of 1853 includes surprisingly few Gothic examples – they were regarded as 'rather stern and angular'. Although the Gothic style is very much associated with Victorian architecture, cabinetmakers and their customers remained surprisingly faithful to Rococo-inspired forms, such as papier-mâché beds, balloon-back chairs and cabinets with curvaceous mirrors attached. In the 'Battle of the Styles' which characterizes the later nineteenth century, the Classical also died hard, with Georgian-inspired pieces making a comeback as the nineteenth century progressed.

CHAPTER 8

Late Victorian

BETWEEN ABOUT 1860 and 1914, two movements originated in England that were to be of international importance: the Aesthetic Movement and the Arts and Crafts Movement. Designers and cabinetmakers continued to search for novelties. E.W. Godwin and Bruce Talbert were profoundly influenced by Japanese applied arts, following the opening up of Japanese trade which resulted from Commodore Perry's visit to that country in 1853. Liberty's sold a chair based on an ancient Egyptian example in the British Museum and Sir Lawrence Alma-Tadema produced 'Etruscan' furniture from Pompeian survivals. Stephen Webb designed a cabinet in the Italian Renaissance revival, echoing Mannerist arabesques, which was executed by Collinson & Lock. At the same time, the Georgian and Regency styles enjoyed a revival, with firms like Wright and Mansfield producing pieces in the Adam style and Edwards and Roberts not only restoring but also making excellent reproductions of Chippendale furniture. William Morris included early Georgian models for chairs in his repertoire, while his lectures inspired a younger generation of designer craftsmen, such as Ernest Gimson and Charles Robert Ashbee.

In the 1860s Charles Bevan was doing much to commercialize the Gothic style, but a reaction against it had set in. Sir George Gilbert Scott, the architect of the gabled and pinnacled Albert Memorial, was to write as early as 1857 in his *Remarks on Secular and Domestic Architecture*, 'The practice of building abbeys for gentlemen's residences is gone'. The 1870s were to see the emergence of the 'Queen Anne Style' with J.J. Stevenson (1831-1908) building his own 'Red House' (1871) in the Bayswater Road, London, in a new style which little resembled the work of Hawksmoor and Vanbrugh, but took its name more from literary sources such as William Thackeray's *Henry Esmond*, subtitled *A Colonel in the Service of Her Majesty Queen Anne*. William Burges, in an article in the *British Architect* (1875) said, 'It has been said and with great truth that the real restorer of medieval art was Sir Walter Scott – in the same way Thackeray, by means of his writing, has made Queen Anne's style popular'. This architecture, very much associated with elementary schools, the Bedford Park development and the Royal Borough of Kensington and Chelsea, consisted of an abundance of gables, moldings and porches and the use of red brick in different tones. It

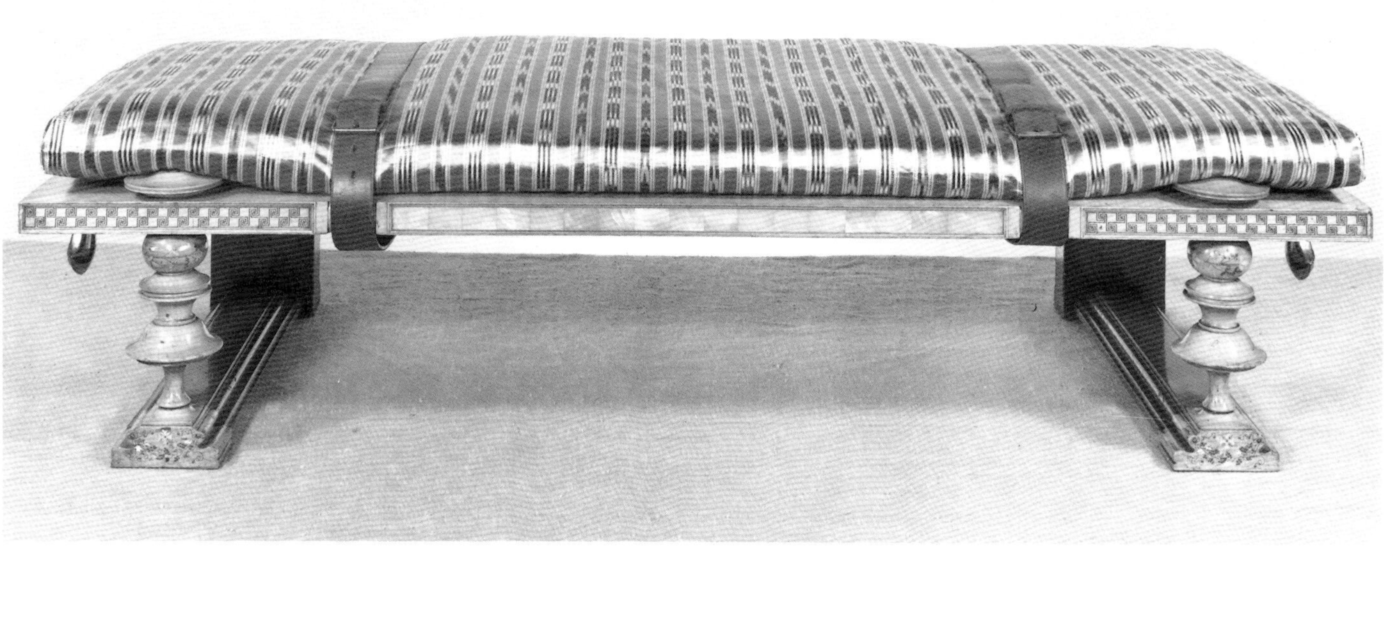

also featured ornamental molded terracotta and the ubiquitous Japanese-inspired sunflower motif – what W. Eden Nesfield called his 'pies'. J.T. Carr, a cultivated property speculator, purchased land and hired E.W. Godwin and Norman Shaw to build Bedford Park in the Queen Anne style.

Charles Eastlake published *Hints on Household Taste* in 1867, outlining his views on taste, including designs for furniture and wallpaper, and providing an early source of 'Art Furniture'. He held that household furniture should be soundly constructed with minimal decoration, and held up as a shining example the honest cartwright's work bereft of unnecessary ornament. Echoing Pugin, he went on to say 'Every article of manufacture should indicate by its general design the purpose to which it will be applied'. Mrs Spofford, a contemporary American writer, described his furniture as, 'Solid wood unvarnished and usually without veneer, made in the simplest manner that conforms to the purpose of the article, with plain uprights and transverses slightly chamfered in the corner'.

ABOVE
Juno Cabinet by Bruce Talbert, made by Jackson & Graham, and exhibited at the Paris Exhibition of 1878.

LEFT
Studio seat in the Pompeian style, designed by Sir Laurence Alma Tadema, about 1893. This featured in a number of his paintings of Roman scenes, such as The Shrine of Venus *and* The Baths of Caracalla, *and was exhibited at The Arts and Crafts Exhibition of 1893.*

7

LEFT
The Golden Bed designed by William Burges in 1879 for the Guest Chamber, Tower House, Melbury Road, London, depicting the Judgment of Paris.

Black and ebonized furniture with small, spindle-shaped balustrades and painted panels became popular, and Collinson & Lock showed their first ebonized cabinet in this style in the 1871 London Exhibition. J. Moyr Smith in his *Ornamental Interiors* (London, 1887) said 'One good painted panel is worth ten thousand times more than all the meretricious carving with which so much of our modern furniture is filled'. Bruce Talbert designed a piece in this style, the Juno Cabinet, which was executed by the design-conscious firm of Jackson & Graham, and exhibited at the 1878 Paris Exhibition. Bruce Talbert (1838-81) was trained as a furniture designer, beginning with the firm of Doveston Bird and Hull. He tended to use low relief and geometric carving, with small panels of birds and enamels to enliven the effect. In 1867 he published *Gothic Forms applied to Furniture* with an approach similar to that of Charles Eastlake, telling readers what pieces of furniture were suitable for which room – massive furniture for the hall, Gothic for the dining room and library and pieces of 'elegance and lightness' for the drawing room.

E.W. Godwin's earlier designs, such as the Northampton Town Hall furniture in 1861, were in the Gothic idiom but his designs for Dromore Castle for the Earl of Limerick, while still retaining Gothic elements, could very much be regarded as the new 'Art Furniture', with Eastlake-inspired economy of ornament. He used the term 'Art Furniture' to describe a series of Japanese-influenced designs that he published in 1877. He worked for the firm Collinson & Lock , designing among other things their shopfront in 1873. He was a close friend of James McNeill Whistler, designing his house in Tite Street and exhibiting furniture painted by the artist at the 1878 Paris Exhibition.

During the 1860s an Adam revival occurred. The firm Wright & Mansfield displayed an Adam cabinet at the Paris 1867 exhibition which was much praised. The *Art Journal Catalogue* stated 'The cabinet manufactured by Messrs Wright & Mansfield of London obtained the only gold medal awarded for British furniture. The foundation is of satinwood, the ornamentation of the panels being of various colored woods, inlaid with marquetry. The panels are filled by Wedgwood plaques. As a specimen of manufacture it is not surpassed by the production of any age or country, and will be memorable as the design of an English artist, Mr Crosse, executed entirely by English architects. It has been purchased for the Museum at South Kensington'. The Mr Crosse mentioned could be

ABOVE

Japanese style buffet by E W Godwin, about 1876, originally in the possession of the designer.

LEFT

E W Godwin's design for a buffet at Dromore Castle, Co. Limerick, 1869, for the 3rd Earl of Limerick, blending Gothic gables with Japanese chrysanthemum motifs.

RIGHT

Adam Style cabinet by Wright and Mansfield, exhibited at the Paris Exhibition of 1867, an early example of the eighteenth century revival.

S. Crosse, architect of Herne Hill. A large sideboard, decorated with ram-head urns and broadly based on a Sheraton design for a cabinet, was displayed at the Philadelphia Centenary exhibition of 1876 and described as 'a magnificent piece of unique work, in the style of the Eighteenth Century, mahogany and inlaid. These fine specimens of material and workmanship commend themselves for special notice'. This helped to begin the eighteenth-century revival in America. Edwards & Roberts was a firm that both dealt in eighteenth-century and Regency originals and made excellent copies which faithfully followed pattern books. Enthusiasts for Regency furniture included Rossetti and Whistler.

The Arts and Crafts Movement, which was to enjoy its heyday from about 1890 until 1910, was largely inspired by the ideals of William Morris and John Ruskin and their distaste for the machine and its degrading effect on the workforce. 'Men living amidst such ugliness,' wrote Morris, 'cannot perceive of beauty and, therefore, cannot express it', Indeed Morris & Co. exhibited an 'Artisan's

LEFT

Adjustable back chair designed by Warrington Taylor after 1866, for Morris & Co, based on a chair seen in Sussex. The Bird tapestry upholstery with which this chair is covered came into production in 1878.

RIGHT

Japanese style screen designed by W E Nesfield and given to Norman Shaw as a wedding present in 1867 by the sculptor and cabinetmaker James Forsyth.

Model Dwelling' in the New Art Museum, at Manchester.

Arthur Heygate Mackmurdo (1851-1942), a designer whose ideas were to be influential in the creation of Art Nouveau style but who was also profoundly influenced by Ruskin, founded the Century Guild in 1882 in order '. . . to render all branches of art the sphere no longer of the tradesman, but of the artist . . .' and to 'restore building, decoration, glass painting, pottery, wood-carving and metal to their rightful place beside painting and sculpture'. Mackmurdo's furniture was exhibited at the Inventions Exhibition of 1885 in London and the Shipperies Exhibition in 1886 in Liverpool. The stand of the Liverpool International Exhibition was adorned with slender columns surmounted with massive cornices and included a large buffet and chair. The *British Architect* of 5 November 1886 'did not altogether like the buffet, with its slender detached pillars, which are in strong contrast to the broad, plain surface of the lower parts and the massive projecting cornice'. The most striking feature about the chair is the tall rail at the top, which is narrower than the back and surmounted with a cornice. Reactions to Century Guild furniture ranged from *The Builder*'s comment on a piano as 'a good unpretending piece of furniture' to *The Cabinetmaker*'s description of tops of chairs like

the one just mentioned as having 'a sharp projecting elbow-splitting cornice'.

The term 'Arts and Crafts' was coined in 1888 by T.J. Cobden Sanderson, who preferred it to 'Combined Arts' as the title for an exhibition of national fine and decorative arts. Walter Crane, the first president of the Arts and Crafts Exhibition Society, echoing Morris who was on the committee, wrote, 'The movement . . . represents in some sense a revolt against the hard mechanical conventional life and its sensibility to beauty (quite another thing to ornament). It is a protest against that so-called industrial progress which provides shoddy wares, the cheapness of which is paid for by the lives of their producers and the degradation of their users'. The Arts and Crafts Exhibition Society had its first exhibition at the New Gallery in Regent Street, London. Subsequent exhibitions held in 1888, 1889, 1890 and 1893 included furniture designed by C.R. Ashbee, Ernest Gimson, the Barnsley brothers, George Jack (Morris's chief cabinetmaker), Charles Voysey and W.R. Lethaby.

Charles Richard Ashbee, more famous for his metalwork designs, was influential in the setting up of the Guild of Handicrafts along with Mackmurdo, Herkomer, Walter Crane and Lewis F. Day. The guild practised woodwork, leatherwork, metalwork and jewelry and exhibited at Arts and Crafts exhibitions. Ashbee designed his mother's house at 37 Cheyne Row, London, called The Magpie and Stump, with the guild doing the work. The dining-room furniture included rush-seated, ladder-backed chairs, and a long table supported by four X-frame legs linked with a stretcher. His most prestigious commission was the redecoration and furnishing, in collaboration with Hugh Baillie Scott, of the drawing room and dining room in the palace at Darmstadt for the Grand Duke of Hesse in 1898. The furniture included leather-embossed high-back chairs, similar to seventeenth-century leather-upholstered seating, and simple, squared-off cabinets, resembling boxes on square legs. In 1902 Ashbee moved with the Guild to Chipping Camden, embarking on an ambitious rehabilitation of cockney workers in rural Gloucestershire. The venture folded by 1907, despite international acclaim, but a number of the workers continued to operate independently.

Ernest Gimson's aim was to produce work that was 'useful and right, pleasantly shaped and finished, good enough, but not too good for ordinary use'. The son of a prosperous Leicester engineer, he was helped by Morris to become articled to J.D. Sedding's architectural office. There he met the Barnsley brothers, Ernest and Sidney, and studied traditional crafts in his spare time. After leaving Sedding's office he traveled to Italy, Greece and Turkey, where he studied Byzantine ornament, which he later incorporated into his inlays. He also learnt chair-turning under Philip Clisset, a chair bodger from Herefordshire who had supplied rush-seated and ladder-backed chairs to the Art Workers' Guild in 1888. At the 1890 Arts and Crafts Exhibition, as part of the firm, he exhibited plasterwork and a drop-front ebony cabinet, based on the sixteenth/seventeeth-century Spanish *vargueño*, whose central motif was a circular floral design, inlaid with mother-of-pearl.

Gimson also helped found the firm of Kenton & Co.,

LEFT

Pet sideboard designed by Bruce Talbert and made by Gillow & Co., and exhibited at the London International Exhibition of 1871. The inscription, translated from Latin, reads 'Better is a dinner of herbs, where love is, than a stalled ox and hatred therewith.'

RIGHT

Cabinet designed by Thomas Collcutt, made by Collinson & Lock and exhibited at the London International Exhibition of 1871; a fine example of 'Art Furniture' with painted panels.

along with the architects William Lethaby, Sidney Barnsley, Mervyn Macartney and Reginald Blomfield 'with the object of supplying furniture of good design and good workmanship'. The firm exhibited furniture at Barnard's Inn in 1891, including a pair of cabinets on stands by Gimson; a wardrobe of Indian walnut by Barnsley – a striking piece with geometrical patterns formed by veneers with grains running in opposite directions; and a revolving rectangular bookcase by Blomfield. The firm disbanded the next year when the various architects reverted to their architectural practices. Gimson moved to the Cotswolds with the Barnsley brothers, renting Pinbury Park from Lord Bathurst.

From 1894 the Barnsleys, particularly Sidney, produced furniture such as ladder-back chairs (chairs the backs of which had a number of rails, making them resemble ladders), large oak dressers and oak chests while Gimson concentrated on plasterwork. In 1902 the group moved their workshop to Sapperton, where Gimson produced metalwork and furniture ranging from the Spanish *vargueño* type to bedsteads with head and foot boards in the waggon-back style. This was a sort of latticework of chamfered verticals and horizontals, the latter undulating towards the centre. Latticework was used on benches, and was repeated on a sideboard displayed at the Arts and Crafts Exhibition of 1916, though on this occasion used as a plate rack at the back of the piece. In 1905 Gimson broke with Ernest Barnsley but continued to operate with his brother Sidney. He exhibited at Debenham & Freebody's department store in 1907, and *The Builder* (December 1907) praised his furniture as being 'not only unexceptionable in taste but thoroughly well made', mentioning 'a chest o' drawers made of English walnut, inlaid in front with a rather conventional floral motif in walnut and cherry' and a 'small cabinet' of 'chevron marquetry'.

Gimson's work was often stark in design, and adorned with pronounced chamfering derived from the art of the wheelwright. Inlay was another mark of his decoration, ranging from simple, alternating contrasts between dark and light woods to elaborate ornamentation, as in the Westminster Cathedral pews. He prided himself on his hands-on experience in making furniture, unlike most designers, and was thoroughly conversant with the materials used. His work was praised by the *Studio Magazine* but *Country Life* felt that it had 'too close a kinship with the packing case'.

Another designer prominent in the Arts and Crafts movement was William Richard Lethaby (1857-1931). He helped found the Art-Workers' Guild in 1884 and with Gimson was one of the leading forces in Kenton & Co. He did not look for a solution in rural Gloucestershire, but rather concerned himself with the improvement of industrial design, being active in the creation of the Design and Industries Association in 1915. Lethaby insisted that

LEFT
Armchair in the Graeco-Roman style designed by Sir Lawrence Alma Tadema and made by Norman Johnstone & Co. in 1884, for the music room of Henry Gurdon Marquand's Madison Avenue mansion in New York.

FAR LEFT
Cabinet on stand designed by C R Ashbee and made by J W Pyment and others, 1903. The inside drawers are decorated with red morocco leather, tooled in gold. Ashbee is harking back to seventeenth-century prototypes such as the Spanish varguēno.

LEFT
Cabinet on a stand by Ernest Gimson, made at the Daneway workshops in 1902. The gilt gesso panels were executed by Gimson himself. Note the arrangement of the grain of the walnut veneer.

ABOVE
Ladderback chair, about 1888, designed and turned on a pole lathe by Gimson himself.

RIGHT
Design for a clock case by C R A Voysey, 1895, for the artist's own use.

'the living stem of building design can only be found by following the scientific method' and that 'the House of the future will be designed as a ship is designed, as an organism which has to function properly in all its parts'. One of his best known pieces of furniture is a massive sideboard from Melsetter House, on the Isle of Orkney, now at the Victoria and Albert Museum.

In Europe Art Nouveau and Jugendstil were the dominating forces; the term Art Nouveau was derived from a gallery of that name opened in Paris in 1895. The style was called 'Jugendstil' in Germany, after the magazine *Jugend*, and 'Stile Liberty' in Italy after the famous shop in London. It was characterized by sinuous curving lines, tendril-like leaf and flower motifs and flowing female figures, and was applied mainly to the decorative arts. British designers such as Arthur Mackmurdo, Charles Voysey, Charles Rennie Mackintosh and Hugh Baillie Scott played their part in forming this style, although their work never achieved the sinuous assymetries of the Belgian designer Victor Horta or the French glassmaker Emile Gallé. An early example by Mackmurdo is the flame-flower motif, used on the title page of his work *Wren's City Churches*, applied to the back of a chair featured in the *Studio Magazine* of 1899, and a satin screen at the

DESIGN FOR A CLOCK CASE TO BE MADE IN WOOD & PAINTED IN OIL COLOUR FULL SIZE
1/2 PLAN LOOKING UP
1/2 PLAN OF TOP
SECTION OF CORNICE
TIME & TIDE WAIT NO·MAN
C.F.A. Voysey. Architect
January 15. 1895.
23. York Place
Baker St. London W.

William Morris Gallery. Striking in two dimensions, it was rather cautious when confined to the back of what is essentially a Neo-Georgian chair.

Charles Voysey (1857-1941) exhibited wallpapers and fabrics at the exhibition of the Arts and Crafts Exhibition Society of 1888 and first showed furniture in 1893. He practised as an architect and included H.G. Wells, E.J. Hornimann and other progressive thinkers among his clients. One of his commissions was an 'improved pub' for the Earl of Ellesmere, who campaigned to abolish drunkenness in the working classes. Unlike Morris, he regarded the machine as a fact of life that might drive out 'the human quality' but could also 'liberate men's minds for more intellectual work'. As a furniture designer he attached great importance to simplicity: 'We cannot be too simple . . . we are too apt to furnish our rooms as if we regarded our wallpapers, furniture and fabrics as far more attractive than our friends'. One of his earliest designs was the Swan chair, a well-proportioned but very stark piece, with extended uprights. Voysey's furniture is typically of plain oak, often decorated with brass strap hinges or flat incised brass panels, with the emphasis on extended uprights, an idea developed from Mackmurdo who used it for his stand at the Liverpool International Exhibition of 1876. More novel items included a hand-painted clock and colored inlay for the doors of a paper case.

Hugh Baillie Scott's first important work was to collaborate with Ashbee in working for the Grand Duke of Hesse at Darmstadt. His bold and simplified style with bright colors was very popular in Europe, particularly Germany, where it was actively promoted by Hermann Muthesius in his three-volume study *Das Englische Haus*. Between 1900 and 1914 Baillie Scott designed furniture and interiors for the Deutsche Werkstätte and the Wertheimer in Berlin. One of his novelties was the Manxman Piano, which concealed the keyboard behind two large and brightly-colored shutters. Perhaps his most eccentric work was a tree-top house called *Le Nid* with accompanying furnishings built for Queen Marie of Romania.

One of the most internationally acclaimed British architects and designers of the late Victorian period was Charles Rennie Mackintosh, whose striking and unorthodox designs won him great acclaim, particularly at a series of international exhibitions held before World War I. After leaving the Glasgow School of Art in 1893, he designed furniture for the Glasgow cabinetmakers Guthrie and Wells. His main Glasgow projects were the new School of Art building and Miss Cranston's Tea Rooms. He was launched onto the international scene when he exhibited Scottish furniture at the Viennese Secession exhibition in 1900, and repeated his success at the Turin exhibition of 1902. His work was illustrated in art periodicals all over Europe, including Russia, and he was particularly admired in Viennese avant-garde circles. His later life was rather anti-climactic, dogged by a difficult nature, heavy drinking and ill health.

The elongated forms of Mackintosh's furniture and wall decoration gave rise to the somewhat derisive nickname 'the Spook School' but what seems bizarre in isolation was often justified by the original context. For example in the long, narrow Glasgow Tea Rooms Mackintosh did not wish his chairs to be overwhelmed, hence the particularly long backs, surmounted with elliptical panels, resembling sentries at the tables. Such rooms were usually painted in black and white color schemes, occasionally relieved with touches of pink and silver. The

LEFT Sideboard designed by W R Lethaby for the dining room at Melsetter House, Hoy, the Orkneys, in 1900.

LEFT Sideboard by C R A Voysey, 1898-1900, part of no longer extant interiors designed by the architect for W Ward Higgs of 23 Queensborough Terrace, Bayswater.

RIGHT Manxman piano by Hugh Baillie Scott, about 1903; the protruding keyboard is deliberately hidden.

chairs ranged from the long and narrow to the more sturdy, with backs reinforced with a series of intersecting verticals and horizontals. Unlike Gimson and the Barnsleys, he put more emphasis on appearance than construction; a particularly elongated chair in the main bedroom of Hill House, Helensburgh was criticized as having 'a seat too small and the joints too weak to support anyone sitting on the chair for more than a very short period'.

While Mackintosh was experimenting with avant-garde forms, Sir Edwin Lutyens was producing his own interpretation of classical and Jacobethan forms, in buildings ranging from Castle Drogo to the Viceroy's house at New Delhi. His furniture designs include a grand piano very much in the Jacobethan style, a safe designed like a cabinet on a stand for Marsh Court and the Napoleon chair. His furniture could be massive, with bulky moldings harking back to the seventeenth century, but his Napoleon Chair, of about 1910, was an elegant piece in the *Style Empire* and actually copied from a portrait of Napoleon. Although the Marsh Court safe has features in common with the Arts and Crafts style, he had little sympathy for the Arts and Crafts movement, describing Ashbee as an 'artist and furniture freakist . . . most to me distasteful'.

Charles Rennie Mackintosh's and Hugh Baillie Scott's designs were internationally acclaimed and the *Studio Magazine* became the bible of the art-conscious European middle classes. Hermann Muthesius, a government architect, was appointed to the German Embassy in London in 1896 to report on the progress of English architecture. On his return to Berlin in 1903, he wrote *Das Englische Haus*, which he published over the next two years. In the years leading up to World War I, however, British furniture design became less innovative, losing

THE DISCOMFITURE OF THE PHILISTINES.

On being presented with artful and crafty Puzzle by Artistic Friend. (Query—Is it the right way up? And, if so, *what is it*?)

RIGHT
Writing desk by C R A Voysey, 1896, part of no longer extant interiors designed by the architect for W Ward Higgs.

LEFT ABOVE
Chair for the Argyle Street Tea Rooms, Glasgow, designed by C R Mackintosh in 1897 and exhibited at the Vienna Secession Exhibition of 1900.

LEFT BELOW
Joke in Punch *magazine, May 1903, satirizing chairs designed by Voysey and others. Note by way of contrast the old-fashioned 'Grecian' sideboard in the background.*

out to Germany, Austria and France. As early as 1899 the Chicago publication *The House is Beautiful* commented: 'England, the mother of the modern decorative movement, now seems likely to give up the leadership she has so firmly held for twenty years'. A growing taste for antiques made English furniture increasingly retrogressive. Heal advertised 'Reproductions of Antique Furniture a speciality' and Liberty's 'Reproductions of 17th century Furniture', knowing that they would sell better. As competition in the furniture trade became more cutthroat, there was increasing reluctance to take on new designs; better to play safe and produce large amounts of what dealers and sale catalogues now call 'Edwardian furniture'. Continental designers admired the English Arts and Crafts movement but they were more successful in marrying their ideas to the machine. At the height of anti-German feeling during World War I, Lethaby and others formed the Design and Industries Association in 1915, modeling themselves on the Deutsche Werkbund, and the Goldsmiths' Hall hosted an exhibition organized by the Board of Trade, of 'German and Austrian articles exhibiting best design'.

CHAPTER 9

Early 20th Century

AT THE end of the 1920s Modernism made its first hesitant appearance in Britain. Modernist buildings and furniture owed little to the five classical orders or to historic revivals; they had to have a function, or at least the semblance of one, be executed in a geometric or severely rectilinear style, and be largely stripped of any ornament. The shape or outline of a piece of furniture was often left to speak for itself. The Modernist style had a gradual effect on English furniture during the inter-war decades, although the reviled Jacobethan style took up 90 per cent of the popular market until World War II, or so Sir Gordon Russell was to claim. The 1920s were remarkably conservative in England, and in a depressed economic climate the mass market was dominated by the reassuringly heavily upholstered three piece suite, consisting of a sofa with two matching armchairs. What made this particularly attractive was the fact that it could often be bought through 'part payment'. At the same time, the opulent French reproduction furniture that relied heavily on ormolu mounts was popular among the newly wealthy middle classes.

In the 1930s materials such as tubular steel and bent ply-

RIGHT
Napoleon chair designed by Sir Edwin Lutyens for his own use, about 1913, taken from a chair used by Napoleon in his study at the Tuileries.

LEFT
Cabinet with drawers of macassar ebony designed by J F Johnson and made by Heal & Son, c 1927.

wood, offering a number of new shapes, were used by innovative firms such as PEL and Isokon. By the end of the 1940s Modernism had taken a leading role, largely through government control of design brought about by dire economic necessity. The Festival of Britain in 1951 served as 'a tonic to the Nation', as it pointed the way to more prosperous times and on a far wider and more democratic scale than at any previous period.

The tendency for English furniture manufacturers in the years leading up to World War I to draw on designs of the past grew even more pronounced in the years that followed. The Omega workshops in Fitzroy Square, largely started by art critic Roger Fry, featured in the *Daily Mail* Ideal Home exhibition of 1913. Omega furnished the Cadena Café in Westbourne Grove and a number of London houses, but its appeal was somewhat limited and the enterprise folded within months of the ending of the war, although Duncan Grant and Vanessa Bell continued to design in this idiom. Whereas the French government strove to harness the creative forces of their designers culminating in the Paris exhibition of 1925, the English concentrated on the Wembley Empire exhibition in 1924, a costly venture that devoted little space to furniture, although it opened designers' and manufacturers' eyes to

a new range of wood from the colonies. Betty Joel was to use materials ranging from African cherry mahogany to Australian silky oak, the latter featuring in the surgery of the eminent eye specialist F.A. Williamson-Noble, including a kidney-shaped desk in this material.

During the 1920s and much of the 1930s all things Tudor, ranging from semi-detached ribbon-development houses to Liberty's Great Marlborough Street facade in London, were in vogue. As David Joel wrote, 'A dining-room in the Jacobean manner with bulbous legs was in 1920 "Just the thing" (and still is in many quarters in 1952)'. The British presented Jacobethan interiors in their pavilion in the Paris Exhibition of 1925, which did little to impress their French hosts. However, the writer of the French catalogue found that Sir Edward Maufe (or rather his wife) had set his pieces out '*disposé fort agréablement. . . d'une inspiration plus actuelle que ceux de la Galerie des Invalides*', (most charmingly . . . more inspired by current tastes than those in the Galerie des Invalides). His white-gold gilt writing desk was a rectangular version of the

LEFT
Wardrobe by the Omega workshops, made in 1916 and said to have been part of a suite of furniture designed by Roger Fry for the apartment of Mme Lala Vandervelde.

RIGHT
Box decorated by Duncan Grant for the Omega Workshops, about 1913-16.

ABOVE
Table, 1918-19, painted by Roger Fry for the Omega Workshops and illustrated in the English edition of Vogue in April 1919.

RIGHT
Dressing table, 1931, in Australian oak with ivory handles by Betty Joel, very much in the Modernist style.

knee-hole desk, the drawers pulled by tassels rather than handles. H.P. Shapland, who wrote the furniture section of the report on the Paris Exhibition for the Department of Overseas Trade, compared it favorably with the cabinet work of Émile-Jacques Ruhlmann, the leading French designer of the day: 'His [Ruhlmann's] cabinet work, wonderful though it is, compares unfavorably with such a piece of furniture as the writing table by Sir Edward Maufe and exhibited in the British Pavilion. This is "essentially right" wood construction.' Indeed it was *la parfaite execution* that was the lesson the English had to teach, according to the French catalogue.

In this period, Maurice Adams produced what he called the George V style, a sort of Neo-Georgian pastiche, which he used on particularly low dressers such as the 'King George' model, exhibited at the Palace of Arts, Wembley, and the 'Queen Mary' model which was shown at Olympia a year later. There followed the 'Coronet', 'Connaught', 'Alexandra', and 'Grosvenor'. Cheaper versions, heavily French polished, were produced by hire purchase firms, which often used fabric to conceal the backs if the timber was of poor quality. Adams also produced furniture in the modern style, such as a large cocktail cabinet in 1933 of ebonized mahogany in the form of a massive, fluted, half-columnar stand mounted in chromium, and a semicircular table with stand above.

Meanwhile the Arts and Crafts tradition continued; Arthur Romney Green worked in the urban environment of Strand-on-the-Green, although his one-time assistant Eric Sharp set up his workshop at Winchester. Carl Malmsten of Sweden, very much an anti-Modernist, was also influenced by the movement, showing hostility to what was to become the dominant and highly exportable trend in his own country. Ernest Gimson died in 1919 and the Daneway workshop folded in 1920, one of the last undertakings being Sidney Barnsley's work on the Memorial Library at Bedales, the progressive public school in Hampshire. Sidney Barnsley died in 1926 and his son Edward took over. His style developed more emphasis on curved outlines, slender uprights and slim inlaid sycamore lines. To English timbers he added Australian black bean and Indian rosewood and padouk.

Peter Waals, the Dutch cabinetmaker employed as foreman at the Daneway works in 1901, set up at Chalford, mostly using Norman Jewson to design his furniture although he did on one occasion co-operate with Voysey. He inherited Gimson's cabinetmakers, as well as clients such as the Earl of Plymouth, providing furniture for his London home and Rodmarton Manor. Other clients included W.H. Smith and Son, W.A. Cadbury, the chocolate manufacturer, and Frank Pick, chairman of London Passenger Transport Board. On Pick's recommendation Waals took up the newly created role of Design Adviser at Loughborough Training College, the post taken over by Edward Barnsley in 1939. Sir Ambrose Heal was an active member of the Art-Workers' Guild, exhibiting in 1899 and 1903 and producing catalogues on *Plain Oak Furniture* (1898) and *Simple Bedroom Furniture* (1899), very much in the Arts and Crafts style, as practised by Gimson and the Barnsleys. Although Heal produced reasonably priced Modernistic furniture designed by Arthur Greenwood and E.W. Shepherd, which helped

BELOW
Smoker's cabinet in ebonized wood with plastic inlay, designed by C R Mackintosh for W J Bassett Howke's house at 78 Derngate, Northampton, in 1916.

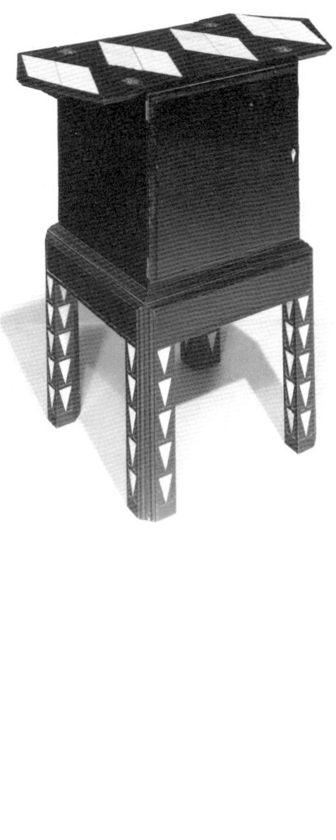

RIGHT
Cocktail cabinet, 1933, by Maurice Adams in ebonized mahogany with chromium mounts. The inside of the doors is designed to carry bottles and the semicircular projection to serve as a table from which to serve drinks. Cocktails were introduced from the USA after World War I.

tide his business over the years of depression, he remained faithful to and provided an important outlet for Arts and Crafts furniture, commissioning among other things a dresser from Sidney Barnsley.

Sir Gordon Russell, who played a vital role in the creation of wartime Utility furniture, was very much part of this tradition. His father founded Russell & Sons Ltd, an antique and restoration business in Broadway, Gloucestershire, and on his return from service in World War I he began to design and make furniture for the family firm, acknowledging his debt to Ernest Gimson: 'Our earliest efforts were made entirely by hand and were directly inspired by the work of Ernest Gimson, many aspects of which I had greatly admired'. This is evident in a bedroom suite made in about 1930, in which every edge of the wardrobe and chest of drawers was chamfered and the handles were in the form of wooden C-shaped handgrips. He borrowed the Gimson-Barnesley waggon-back ornament for the backs of a set of dining chairs in 1924, and applied their principles of making use of local materials with a chest of drawers for David Lloyd George made from a holly tree growing in his garden. A walnut cabinet inlaid with ebony and laburnum and loosely based on seventeenth-century English examples won a gold medal at the Paris Exhibition of 1925. He put his emphasis on handwork, writing 'Handwork enables the worker to get to grips with his material and collaborate with it in a way that is infinitely more difficult if he is operating a machine.' He used Edgar Turner, an employee of the family firm, and Harry Gardiner, previously of the smithy at Daneway, to execute his designs.

After about 1925 Russell introduced machinery in the workshops, his aim being 'to teach the machine manners'. His work in the 1930s consisted of simple bold shapes, particularly in his desks with curved (not quite kidney-shaped) or rectangular tops. In a trade catalogue he stressed the importance of perfect quality of materials, as flaws would show up more easily on machine-made furniture. His designs also included radio cabinets for Murphy Radios, plain rectangular boxes set on plain stands with squared off legs, one particular example being not unlike Gimson's *vargueños*.

LEFT
Writing desk, about 1925, in white-gold gilt, designed by Sir Edward Maufe, made by W Rowcliffe and exhibited at the Paris exhibition of 1925.

LEFT
Chair designed by Sir Ambrose Heal and made by William Jones of Heal & Son for the Paris Exhibition of 1914. Note the chair back, modeled on waggon-sides, characteristic of the work of Ernest Gimson and Sidney Barnsley.

BELOW
Writing desk in oak, designed by Sir Ambrose Heal in 1928 and made by Heal & Son in 1929; one of the 'signed edition series'.

The Modernist style began to appear in England in the late 1920s. In 1928 Paul Follot and Serge Chermayeff decorated sixty rooms for Waring and Gillow, as part of the reorganization of the firm's decoration department to display the more progressive continental design to the English. The most famous is the dining room, with the sideboard and dining table in bold, simple forms curving at the ends, echoing Shapland's statement in the report on the Paris Exhibition: 'The French have always regarded the curved line in furniture as the line of beauty'. The chairs are playfully reminiscent of Louis Seize examples, but stripped of pastiche ornament. 'Lord Waring's belief in the new movement' it was stated, 'should have important reactions on the furnishing industries in the future'.

The Wall Street Crash of 1929 left the buying public with less money to spend, but the Exhibition of Swedish Decorative Art in 1931 at Dorland Hall provided attractively designed furniture in bare rooms which at the time seemed healthier – and was also cheaper. The simple and highly economical elegance of the pieces, whether in the crafts tradition of Carl Malmsten or the modern functionalist style of Eskil Sundahl, struck the right note. Malmsten's exhibits included an inlaid cabinet, chest and several bureaux, one of which echoed English examples of the late eighteenth century. Sundahl exhibited library furniture, the chairs of which were sprung with Knoll's coil springs, which were to have a great impact in England in the form of the Gossip chair. The editor of the *Architectural Review* accounted for the success of Swedish design by observing that Sweden had been a neutral country and could continue traditions uninterrupted, that there was a far closer degree of co-operation between designers and manufacturers than in England and that the Swedish royal family took an active role in design, producing examples themselves.

In 1933 Alvar Aalto, the leading Finnish designer, exhibited his bentwood and laminated plywood furniture at the London store of Fortnum and Mason. This included the famous Chair 41, designed between 1930 and 1933 for his Paimio Sanitorium. The arms and legs formed a continuous loop of bent plywood and the seat a continuous strip of that material, curling over at the top and bottom. The *Architectural Review* of 1933 was enthusiastic, praising the 'cheap and seemly furniture which is comfortable, light and easy to move . . .', and concluding that 'for England it may at last spell death to the fake "Queen Anne."'

Marcel Breuer achieved a similar effect with tubular steel to that of Aalto with bentwood, fusing the uprights, legs and arms of a chair into one by bending this metal in different directions. Breuer was a former teacher of the

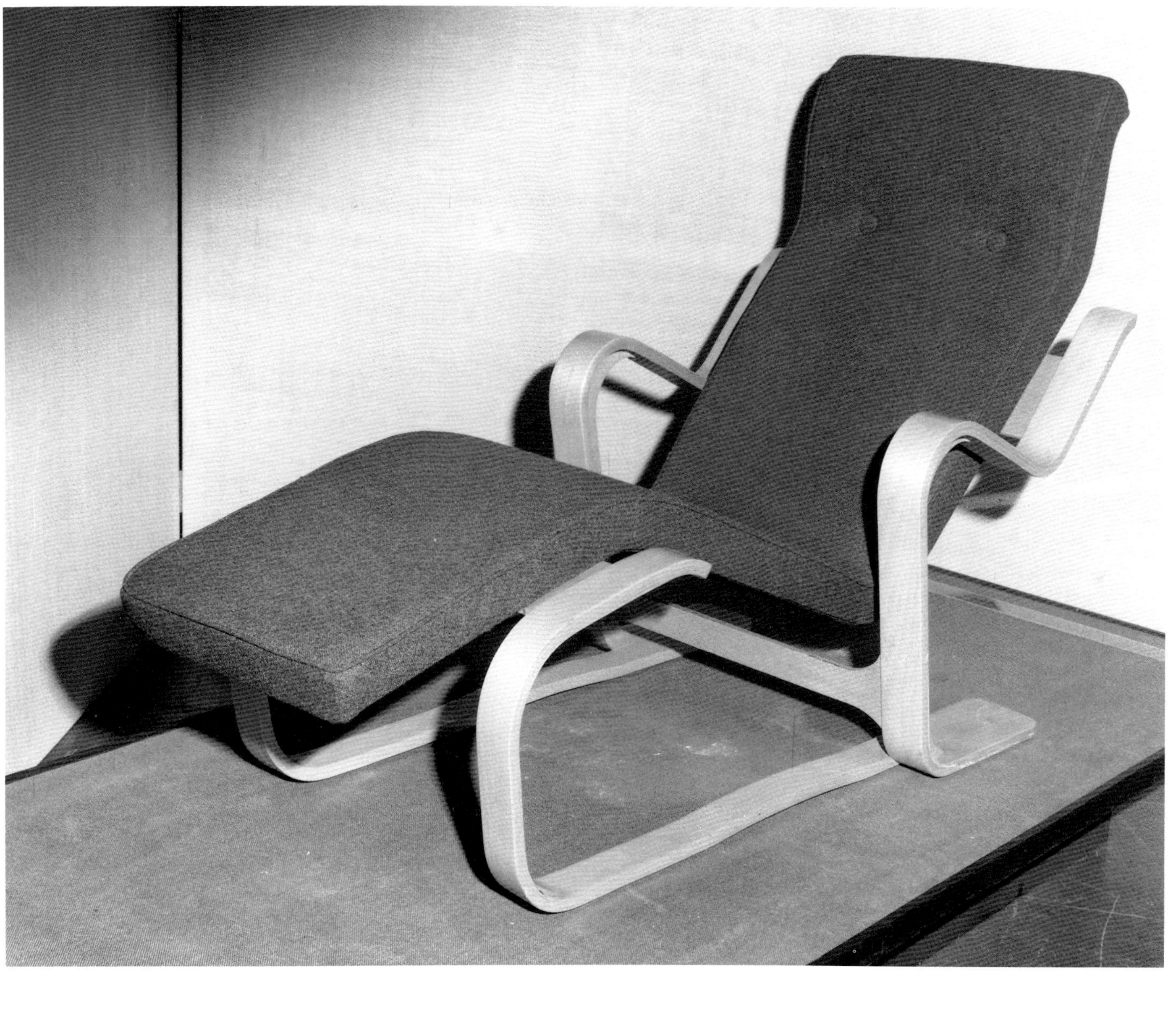

LEFT *Long chair, 1936, designed by Marcel Breuer for Isokon Furniture. The chair frame is of bent plywood and, although made of several pieces of wood, gives the appearance of a continual curve, like the tubular steel furniture he designed for the Bauhaus.*

ABOVE *PEL dining table and chairs, 1933-36, illustrated in* Design for Today *(1933) as being designed by Messrs Joseph and used in the offices of the Prudential Insurance Company.*

German Bauhaus School, one of the main sources of Modernism, which was founded by Walter Gropius in 1919 and dissolved in 1933. He came to England in 1935 and worked on bent plywood with Jack Pritchard of Isokon Ltd. His works for this firm range from chairs in the traditional form of separate seat, legs and back to the 'long chair', with plywood body and legs of bent plywood following a continuous curve, at least in appearance, like his tubular steel furniture. Plywood had been developed mainly in Finland and its commercial success rested not only on its low price but also its resistance to warping and shrinkage.

One designer very much concerned with new materials and their opportunities was Ernö Goldfinger, a Hungarian architect, who moved to London from Paris in 1935. He used plywood, bakelized (from bakelite, an early form of plastic) paper and tubular steel on his chairs. One such design, with a plywood back and seat linked by two strategically bent pieces of tubing and an adjustable back, has been repeated on countless office chairs. In his book *British Furniture To-Day* (London, 1951), he showed great interest in the theories of the Swedish Dr Bengt Akerblom, author of *Standing and Sitting Posture*, on the posture of the human body and how furniture should best be designed to suit it. He also concerned himself with practical problems of contemporary living, such as the storage of clothes and kitchen equipment. One poster he designed for the ABCA exhibition 'Planning Your Kitchen' was entitled *All Details are Important*. 'Jazzy knobs', we are told, 'collect dust'.

The opportunities offered by tubular steel were taken up by the firm PEL, a subsidiary of Tube Investments, who borrowed from continental designers such as Mar-

ABOVE
Stacking chair with adjustable back, about 1930, designed by Ernö Goldfinger. Goldfinger strove to reconcile chair design with the natural human sitting posture.

cel Breuer and Mies Van der Rohe and made tubular furniture for a fashion-conscious market, although their products provoked jibes about 'operating theatre tables'. Their first commission was the furnishing of Broadcasting House, London, soon followed by the provision of equipment for a number of smart hotels such as Claridges and the Savoy in London and the Metropole in Brighton. Tubular steel was admirably suited to the mass production of stacking chairs for canteens and offices, while Breuer's idea of suspending desk drawers from bent tubes was developed by Welles Coates for PEL. Welles Coates, a designer of Canadian origin, founded Isokon with Jack Pritchard for 'the application of the modern functional design to houses, flats, furniture and fittings' and his work ranged from radio design and the BBC sound studios to flats consisting of built-in furniture, such as the Lawn Road flats, one of which was exhibited at the Dorland Hall art exhibition of 1933.

Another designer aware of the possibilities of tubular steel was Denham MacLaren, who operated from a showroom first in Davies Street and then in Grosvenor Street during the early 1930s. He provided tubular steel seating and tables for the London flat of G.H. Saxon Mills in about 1932. He also made a glass-topped circular table, with three thin section legs linked by curved tubular steel, for the flat of a Mrs Tollenaar in Sloane Street in about 1934. He was interested in the opportunities presented by glass, using sheets of it for the frame of his Zebra Chair (so called because of the zebra pattern upholstery) and also providing a rough-cut glass surface for a table-top in Mr Saxon Mills's flat.

An innovation with widespread appeal was the Gossip Chair, a wooden-armed lightly-upholstered fireside chair which could serve as a substitute for the heavily upholstered three piece suite. Wilhelm Knoll, a German de-

LEFT
Folding screen The Blue Screen, *about 1913, painted by Duncan Grant.*

RIGHT
Folding screen, about 1928, by Adrian Paul Allinson, depicting a series of allegorical scenes concerning the arts.

signer, developed tension springs which replaced the steel coils of earlier upholstered chairs and were manufactured by Parker Knoll of High Wycombe. The tyre firm Dunlop developed Dunlopillo, a latex rubber foam that was to be widely used for car and bus seats as well as for wartime aircraft. Other innovations included the use of glass to cover whole walls in one-room flats, and fabrics such as vitrolite, an opaque glass with a smooth face and ridged back enabling it to be fixed to a mastic compound. The problem presented by curved surfaces was solved by vitroflex, a closely woven fabric onto which small squares or rectangles of thin mirror were placed. Oliver Hill designed the Pilkington Bros stand at the Dorland House exhibition of 1933, including furniture made from curved sheets of glass, a mosaic floor and panels of ribbed and obscured mirror. Paul Nash designed a bathroom for Tilly Losch with panels of metallic purple, pale rose and black glass. The use of laminated woods made larger doors and built-in cupboards possible, resulting in the gradual disappearance of the wardrobe. Improvements in plumbing and the concentration of washing arrangements in the bathroom made the bedchamber washstand and chamber pot obsolete.

Utility furniture was developed during World War II, at

ABOVE
Table made of glass and chrome, 1931, designed by Denham MacLaren for the Sloane Street flat of Mrs Tollenaar.

RIGHT
Utility cupboard, about 1950, made by Maples and, according to their trade catalogue of that date, an indispensable part of a dining recess 'furnished in typical New Zealand manner'.

RIGHT
Zebra chair, 1931, in glass with zebra skin, by Denham MacLaren, made when he was working for Arundell Clarke, one of the few Modernist interior decorators of the early 1930s.

a time of acute shortages not only of materials but also of domestic furniture lost in air raids. Although initially dubbed 'cardboard furniture' by the popular press and designed in the Modernist stye, it became popular because of its reasonable price and good quality. This was a notable instance of government-controled design. On the Initiative of Hugh Dalton, President of the Board of Trade, a committee was set up to look into the problem of supplying furniture, with Gordon Russell playing the most active role. H.J. Cutler and Edwin Clinch of High Wycombe were appointed designers and some thirty types of furniture were worked on. A form of Modernist design was adopted which was regarded, much to Russell's satisfaction, as too conservative by progressives and too avant-garde by the furniture trade. Veneered hardboard was considered a useful substitute for plywood. A Brains Trust was set up at Toynbee Hall in order to listen to public comments and find out what was wanted. The Utility Furniture Panel included architects like Brian O'Rorke and Grey Wornum and also Jacques Groag, a Czech pupil of Adolf Loos. When the first range appeared it included a dining table and chairs, sideboard, kitchen cabinet, and bedroom suite comprising a bed, wardrobe, tallboy and dressing table. In 1944 all-steel bedsteads were included and a year later the Cotswold and Chiltern ranges were introduced, no doubt with the great masters like Gimson in mind. 'Simplicity and refinement of design' was the aim, together with a low price and high quality. With the added bonus of Utility furniture being exempt from purchase tax, this assured the popularity of a line that continued until 1952. In fact, as Russell said, 'the ubiquitous tastelessness of popular furniture has been replaced by standardized good taste'.

'Contemporary' furniture emerged in Britain in the late 1940s based on Scandinavian examples, and books, magazines and television programmes helped extol the virtues of this style. New towns and housing programmes gave additional impetus to 'contemporary' designs, and wartime technology, particularly from aircraft, was applied to domestic furniture. Molded ply had been used for Mosquito fuel tanks and synthetic adhesives had been developed; one of the sections of the exhibition called

'Britain Can Make It', hosted by the Victoria and Albert Museum, was 'From a Spitfire to a Saucepan'. Metal was used for the chassis of chairs and settees and for the frames on which sideboards were suspended, so as to avoid drawing on depleted stocks of timber. New laminated plastics and anodized aluminum, particularly for shelves and tabletops, permitted a large range of bright colors.

The most optimistic exhibition of this period was the Festival of Britain of 1951, the centenary of the Great Exhibition of 1851. The Council for Industrial Design, which had been established in 1944, produced a stocklist that included 1620 items of furniture. Some months before the exhibition, a series of panels was appointed by the industries concerned to make recommendations as to which were to be included or rejected. Designers on various 'Homes and Gardens' projects then consulted the stocklist for the pieces best suited to their themes. Furniture designed by Ernest Race and Robin Day was particularly popular. The slender, light, but strong aluminum chairs, such as Race's Springbok and Antelope, used at the various cafés and restaurants of the Festival offered a pleasant contrast to the more boxy Utility style. Robin Day produced the Pre-form Chair with the back and arms made from one piece, a variation of which also served as restaurant furniture. Rubber sponge developed by Dunlop was used more widely, often replacing Knoll's tension springs.

Throughout the 1950s space became at even more of a premium. Despite ambitious housing schemes, shortages remained and many of the interiors exhibited during the decade showed various ways of saving space. The room divider made its appearance, helping to create a greater sense of privacy, while Gomme of High Wycombe provided their G-Plan furniture as well as unit storage. Robin Day won a Council for Industrial Design award for his settee bed in the late 1950s and his interiors featured in an article on 'At Home with the Days' in an Ideal Home Yearbook. Alison and Peter Smithson produced a 'House of the Future' at the Ideal Home Exhibition, which included a number of unorthodox chairs such as the Petal Chair and the Saddle Chair, while the Pogo Chair, with a hard plastic back and seat, both bent down the middle like an open book and linked by a single metal tube, was to serve as a dining chair.

Following the Scandinavian example, furniture tended

to be bought more as individual items rather than as a three-piece suite. In addition, plants, pictures and small decorative items became important. Ornament became more abstract and geometric, with repetitive series of stars, circles and hexagons used on cupboard doors, while Robert Hermitage used a router to create a repeated machine-made pattern on a sideboard. Not only were the designs by Robin Day and Ernest Race at the Festival of Britain highly popular but the craze for Do-It-Yourself helped consolidate the modern style. Such pieces as bookshelves, lamps, plant-stands, coffee-tables, and trolleys were particularly suited to simple construction. The increasing affluence of the British family in the 1950s and the rejection of wartime and post-war austerity meant that the latest fashions in furniture, instead of being confined to the very rich, were now becoming available to the masses. As Ernest Race said, 'Perhaps the most significant development of the last year has come not so much from the manufacturers, retailers and designers but from the public itself'.

LEFT
Kidney-shaped desk designed and made by Betty Joel for the consulting room of the eye specialist F A Williamson-Noble.

ABOVE
Antelope chair by Ernest Race, 1950, manufactured by Race Furniture Ltd from 1950 onwards.

LEFT
Springbok chair by Ernest Race, 1950, made with plastic-covered springs, and manufactured by Race Furniture Ltd from 1950 onward. Like the Antelope chair, this was designed for outdoor use at the Festival of Britain.

RIGHT
Pogo plastic chair, 1956, perspex seat and back rest and satin-coated chrome frame, designed by Peter and Allison Smithson for the 'House of the Future', the Ideal Home Exhibition of 1956.

CHAPTER 10

Late 20th Century

FURNITURE OF the 1960s is very much associated with Pop culture; the discovery of low-cost synthetic materials such as acrylic and fibre glass allowed designers ever more freedom in forming new shapes for their furniture. The aim was to create an instant impact like that of the latest pop record, largely intended for a young market, by now more affluent, self-confident and assertive. As far as the mass as opposed to Pop market was concerned, the British furniture industry became standardized and increasingly automated during the 1960s. Manual labor was drastically cut and white wood furniture increasingly imported to be finished in British factories. With the growth of Do-it-Yourself, the packaging of rectangular components saved space and as a result mass-produced furniture took on a more boxy appearance. It was increasingly assembled at home from large pieces of chipboard, a cheap substitute for plywood. The emphasis was on low to medium priced products, many of them imitating Scandinavian and Italian examples, albeit in a somewhat tame British manner. In the 1970s and 1980s furniture developed in many directions, including the crafts revival; Post-Modernism, typified by the architecture and furniture designs of Charles Jencks; Minimalism, found in the stark simplicity of Jaspar Morrison; and the historical revival found in the furniture of Robert Adam.

The consumer market, particularly the young with more money in their pockets, had begun to expand in the 1950s and increased further in the 1960s. Pop furniture, along with pop music and pop fashions, took on an instantaneous quality that could be discarded once it had

LEFT
Dining table designed in 1936 by Marcel Breuer for the Isokon Furniture Company. As the table was too large to be made out of a single piece of plywood, the legs are joined to the top by means of supporting fins.

ABOVE RIGHT
Chair and stool by David Colwell, c. 1983, this time more in the spirit of the Crafts Revival.

RIGHT
Contour chair by David Colwell, 1968; acrylic sheet supported on a steel rod frame, and an example of Sixties experimenting with synthetic materials.

gone out of style. Before the oil crisis of 1973 'Throw-away Culture' was a catch-phrase. At the same time the 'packaged good taste' of Terence Conran emerged; his shop Habitat was opened in the Fulham Road, London, in 1964 where he sold furniture he designed himself. A year earlier he designed Mary Quant's highly successful Bazaar in Knightsbridge, and his press release described Habitat as 'a shop for the switched-on people selling not only our own furniture and textiles but other people's too. It's functional and beautiful'. Conran offered packaged good taste for those who wanted to buy a complete lifestyle, selling bentwood furniture, tin enamelware and kitchen utensils, particularly 'French Farmhouse', for those who cooked food based on Elizabeth David's recipes. For those of the middle classes who wanted to play safe, department stores such as Peter Jones and Whiteleys' sold quality reproduction or contemporary furniture, while chainstores like Time Furnishings and John Perrings catered for the mass market until the mid 1960s.

As standardization continued the chair took on a new importance, providing designers with the greatest scope for originality, as the Whitechapel Art Gallery Exhibition *Modern Chairs 1918-1970* in the summer of 1970 showed. The increasingly ephemeral nature of furniture, which could be made from petrol-based materials such as plastics and acrylics (before the 1973 oil crisis), made instant impact possible for the designer and, more importantly, for the potential buyer, particularly the mass youth market. In the magazine *Harper's Bazaar* in February 1965, Barbara Griggs referred to the '. . .enjoy-it-today-sling-it-tomorrow philosophy. . . uninterested in quality and workmanship as long as design is witty and new'. There was a great demand for furniture with bright colors, such as Max Glendenning's plywood chair from the Maxima range, made of broad flat components resembling jigsaw pieces (described by Michael Webb in *Industrial Design*, October 1967 as 'Charles Rennie Mackintosh taking a trip'), and Bernard Holdaway's plywood pieces for Hull Traders, such as a flower-shaped table, round the petals of which cylindrical chairs fitted. David Colwell designed the Contour Chair, the concave seat of which was made from a sheet of acrylic heated in an oven and pressed down with a rectangular stamp at the end of a pneumatic stamp.

The new synthetic materials could be made into any shape and European, particularly Italian, designers exploited the opportunities to the full with world-wide im-

LEFT
Column of drawers of plied birch, 1978, designed by John Makepeace and made by him at Parnham House, derived from an earlier version exhibited at the Craftsman's Art in 1973.

RIGHT
Modernist bathroom furniture in Claridge's Hotel, London.

pact. Blow-up furniture, developed from Zanotta's Italian Blow Chair, was popular and Conran marketed his as 'a perfect picnic chair'. Another highly popular Italian import, indispensable to Bedsitter land, was the *sacco*, a leather bag, designed by Gatti, Paolini and Teodoro in about 1968, which was stuffed with up to 12 million polystyrene granules (or so the manufacturers claimed!) and was described as the Chair of 1001 Nights (1000 positions by day and 1 by night). Designers like Archigram advocated minimalist furniture, with dining-table and chairs sunk into the floor, preferably one 'made hard enough to dance on and soft enough to sit on'. Roger Dean designed the Sea Urchin with '. . . a vague notion of a chair one could do anything with; one could sit on it in any position, and approach it from any direction'. In his case, the stuffing was polyurethane foam rather than polystyrene beads.

The importance of easy packaging gave rise to the knock-down chair such as Nicholas Frewing's Flexible Easy Chair and Jean Schofield's and John Wright's C1 chair. Peter Murdoch's paper chair was made possible by

using five different laminations and three different papers. As the Whitechapel Art Gallery Exhibition catalogue said, 'With a unit cost measured in pennies, a chair of this kind can be completed on one machine at the rate of one per second, and can be shipped in a minimal volume – 800 chairs in a pile no more than four feet in height'. This design won awards both in Britain and America. References to the need for 'marketing development' hint at the more conservative ways of English manufacturers, who were not interested in making this chair – it ended up being imported from America.

Yet again historical styles enjoyed a vogue. This time it was Victoriana, largely made popular through boutiques like 'I was Lord Kitchener's Valet' in Carnaby Street, London, and the 1920s and 1930s. It became fashionable to buy cheap Victorian and Edwardian furniture in second-hand shops and liven it up by painting it. Binder, Edwards and Vaughan made designs based on barge and fairground decoration for the sophisticated, and Habitat sold a stencil kit to help amateurs. Firms such as Zeev Aram and Associates, OMK, Plush Kicker and Minale Tattersfield provided Modernist black leather and tubular steel revivals, such as OMK's version of Marcel Breuer's Wassily Chair or Plush Kicker's adaptation of 1930s PEL furniture, designed by Peter Wigglesworth and R.V. Exton in 1968.

Avant-garde office furniture design was pioneered in America by architects like Frank Lloyd Wright and manufacturers like the Art Steel Furniture Company at the beginning of the twentieth century, and Charles Eames was responsible for a number of post-war classics. In Britain more progressive managements in the 1930s such as the BBC had bought tubular furniture by PEL, and during the more affluent post-war decades Hille exploited the possibilities offered, producing the Status range, to the designs of Robin Day. After World War II British manufacturers such as Hille sought opportunities in contract furnishing, and his licence to sell the furniture of Herman Miller, the great American firm, no doubt increased his awareness. Robin Day, the main designer for Hille, came up with stacking chairs such as the 1950 Hillestak chair and the 1953 Q-Stack chair, both of plywood. The Status range included a series of virtually identical desks that made allowances for the variations of organizational hierarchies; for example, senior managers were provided with 'modesty panels' for greater privacy, the middle echelons an open knee-hole and secretaries a single pedestal. In 1961 Day produced the Polypropylene chair which, though similar to Charles Eames's fibreglass chairs, used polypropylene, a lightweight and flexible plastic discovered by the Italian chemist Giulio Natta. John Lewak and Alan Turville designed Hille's storage wall system for offices as well as hotels and homes. The walls, shelves, doors and lighting tracks were all part of

ABOVE
Child's paper chair of polythene-coated laminated paper, designed by Peter Murdoch, 1964. Part of the 'throw-away' culture, this chair could be assembled from one piece of paper.

RIGHT
An advertisement in House and Garden *magazine, November 1959, for the Hille bed-settee, designed by Robin Day and given the Design Centre Award in 1957.*

the same unit, which consisted of a series of vertical panels clipped to rolled steel channels, fixed to the permanent, structural walls.

The most significant recent development in England has been the Nomos furniture developed by Norman Foster of Foster Associates, famous for high tech buildings such as the Hong Kong and Shanghai Bank and the Sainsbury Centre for the Visual Arts, Norwich. Tecno, the Italian firm, commissioned Foster to develop a new range of office furniture. On the premise that space was at a premium they based everything around the table, raising storage and lighting above it. Rather than boxing up the cables needed for new information technology hardware, they managed to thread them through a spine of plastic vertebrae without the need to remove plugs. They aimed for a basic framework rather than a fixed solution, saying they were producing 'an inventory, not a system'; 'Nomos is not a Swiss Army Knife'.

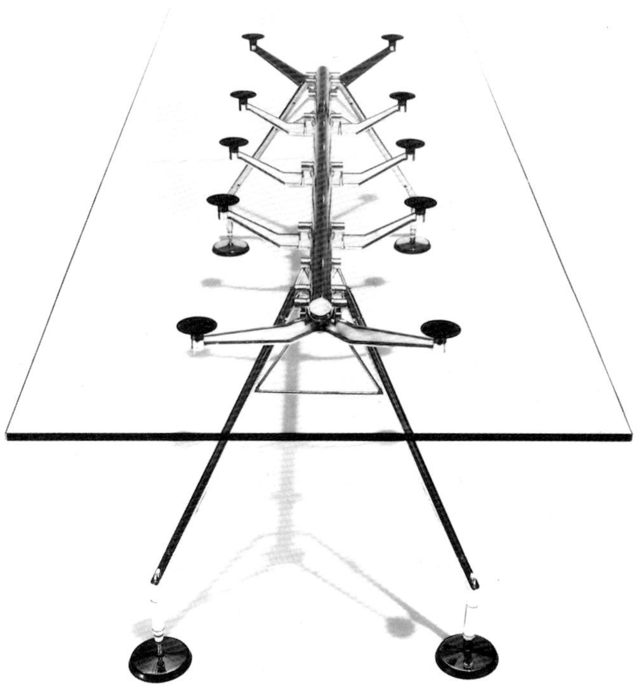

ABOVE
Nomos table, 1986, designed by Norman Foster in chromium-plated steel with metal and glass fittings and manufactured by Tecno.

RIGHT
Polypropylene stacking chair, 1963, designed by Robin Day and given the Design Centre Award in 1965.

In the 1980s in Sweden a minimalist approach to furniture design became more common, largely brought about by a concern with the environment and the wastage of natural resources. Johan Huldt and Jan Dranger of the firm Innovator developed a series of knock-down tubular frames covered with canvas for easy maintenance. Their economy is reflected by Jasper Morrison, an English designer, who lays stress on simplicity and expressiveness. He believes in economy both of style and technique, an example being his low chair, a lyrically curved plywood frame supporting a plywood skin and resting on chrome steel legs, the only decoration being two back feet. His Thinking Man's chair is a simple combination of strip and tubular steel with the terminations of the arms faintly reminiscent of Voysey. Other examples include a free-form plywood desk for Neotu in Paris which is characteristically economical with materials and design, as is Nick Allen's stool, a stark piece which is a mixture of classical design and the ancient Egyptian style Thebes stool sold by Liberty's during the 1880s.

Robert Adam has produced furniture that imitates late eighteenth-century neoclassical designs. In contrast, André Dubreuil, a Frenchman who has lived and trained in England for 20 years, adopts a more flamboyant approach, reacting against Modernism and often drawing his inspiration from the past, possibly influenced by his time spent as an antique dealer. Both his Paris chair and Spine chair are highly individualistic, a quality that he finds congenial about English design. Ron Arad, who came to England from Israel in 1973, makes metal furniture which has been described as 'welded steel sculpture'. He believes in 'creative salvage', an example being a seat from a Rover 2000 rescued from a scrap yard and set on tubular steel mounts. His work is marketed as 'Art Furniture', with a price to match.

Charles Jencks, the American Post-Modernist architect based in London, has designed furniture for his own house which borrows ideas from classical and Egyptian architecture, such as a series of dice tables shaped like the triglyph of the Doric order and an Egyptian-style telephone kiosk. Other motifs include the sunburst, which forms the back of his Spring chair and Sun chair. He indulges in humorous puns like the Window chair, with its

back in the form of a window and all four legs joined by stretchers in a window formation.

The 1970s and 1980s have been marked by a crafts revival. In 1971 Lord Eccles, the then Paymaster-General, set up the Crafts Advisory Committee under the wing of the Council of Industrial Design, laying stress on the 'artist-craftsman' whose work should be promoted and supported by government grants. In 1973 'The Craftsman's Art', a highly successful exhibition, was held at the Victoria and Albert Museum, and *Crafts* magazine was founded. Designers became more interested in applying manufacturing techniques to the craft workshop, but on a smaller scale, which meant that they could control the methods and quality of the actual production. David Mellor set up his cutlery factory in Sheffield; Frank Thrower founded Dartington Glass; and Peter Miles and Ronald Carter made Peter Miles Furniture. In 1977 John Makepeace opened the John Makepeace School of Craftsmen in Wood, funded by the Parnham Trust. He concerned himself with matters ranging from technology to forestry, acquiring the nearby Hooke Park forest to develop the use of small roundwood to complement batches of designer furniture of expensive timber. Makepeace's aim has been to emphasize the skills that are needed to enable students to make a living as self-employed designers. He has eschewed the ruralism of Ashbee or Gimson but applied industrial methods to handcrafts, drawing advanced metalwork ideas from firms linked to Westland Helicopters in nearby Yeovil. David Colwell, who made the Contour chair, is based in Wales and works in the craft revival idiom, an example being a chair in the form of a deckchair, the general flow of which terminates in a footstool, and a round table supported by triangularly-linked legs.

Heroic attempts have been made to improve machine-produced design in Britain by designers and architects all too aware that the French dominated design in the 1850s,

ABOVE
Rib chair, 1986; epoxy-coated frame and vinyl upholstery, designed by Paul Chamberlain and Peter Christian.

LEFT
Stool, 1987-88, with steel frame and stained sycamore seat, designed by Nick Allen and harking back to Liberty's Theban chair from 100 years earlier.

LEFT
Steel Paris chair, 1988, designed by André Dubreuil. The speckled effect was achieved with a blow torch.

BELOW
Spring chair, 1984, designed by Charles Jencks and similar to furniture in his house in Holland Park.

the Germans and Austrians up to World War I, the French again up until World War II, and the Americans, Scandinavians and Italians since. In the years following the Festival of Britain, Robin Day, Ernest Race and Alison and Peter Smithson produced highly innovative furniture which could be made on a mass scale. In spite of the Anglomania that resulted, the Swinging Sixties did not produce a furniture Renaissance in this country. What forms and shapes English designers could provide, their Finnish and Italian counterparts could do better. The instinct to play safe reasserted itself with regard to the latest trends, and revivalist styles tended to offer the most attractive solution. The English craft tradition has a way of reasserting itself, and providing one of the most fertile sources for innovative design. From the Great Exhibition to the Arts and Crafts Exhibition Society, from the Festival of Britain to the Crafts Revival: one can detect similar swings of the pendulum in the form of a reaction against mass production, whether through nineteenth-century socialistic ideals or the late twentieth-century belief that 'Small is Beautiful'.

Index

Figures in *italics* refer to illustrations

Acknowledgments

The publisher would like to thank Design 23 who designed this book, Moira Dykes, the picture researcher, Jessica Orebi Gann, the editor, and Pat Coward who prepared the index. Many thanks also to the Picture Library at the Victoria and Albert Museum for all their help and patience. All photographs were supplied Courtesy of the Board of Trustees of the Victoria and Albert Museum, except for the following:
The British Architectural Library, Royal Institute of British Architects: pages 103, 120 (below), 129
Courtesy of His Grace, the Duke of Buccleuch and Queensberry, KT, Boughton House: page 55 (top)
Courtesy of the Castle Howard Estate, York: page 90
Devonshire Collection, Chatsworth. Reproduced by Permission of the Chatsworth Settlement Trustees: page 65
Harewood House, Property of the Earl and Countess of Harewood/ Photo Jim Kershaw: page 15 (below)
By Permission of the Dean and Chapter of Hereford: page 21
Courtesy of Hille/House and Garden: page 154 (below)
Angelo Hornak: pages 152-153
By Permission of the Marquess of Cholmondeley, Houghton, Norfolk/Angelo Hornak: page 61
Courtesy of the Master and Fellows, Magdalene College, Cambridge: page 45
The National Trust Photographic Library pages 7, 10-11, 14 (top)/ Angelo Hornak, 14 (below)/Horst Kolo, 31 (top), 35 (top)/John Betnell, 38, 49 (both), 50, 60 (left)/AC Cooper, 64 (top), 68, 72 both, 73/Mark Fiennes, 75 and 76-77/Andrew Haslam, 101 (top)/AC Cooper
The Punch Archive: page 132 (below)
Copyright the Trustees of the John Soane Museum: page 82
By Kind Permission of the Marquis of Tavistock, and the Trustees of the Bedford Estates: page 69 (left)
Courtesy of Temple Newsam House, Leeds: page 76
By Courtesy of Trinity Hall, Aberdeen: page 40
Trinity College, Cambridge, University Library: page 19
By Courtesy of the Dean and Chapter of Westminster: page 22, 23 (top)